THE
CHILTERN HUNDREDS

A COMEDY IN THREE ACTS

BY

WILLIAM DOUGLAS HOME

TO
MR. COLLINGWOOD
My Father's Butler and My Friend

SAMUEL FRENCH

LONDON
NEW YORK TORONTO SYDNEY HOLLYWOOD

Please note our NEW ADDRESS:

Samuel French Ltd
52 Fitzroy Street London W1P 6JR
Tel: 01 - 387 9373

AUTHOR'S NOTE

I wish to acknowledge the invaluable assistance of Archibald Batty (at that time Reader for the firm of H. M. Tennent Ltd.), who, with infinite tact, persuaded me to cut certain scenes and to re-write others in the play—before production—and still remained my friend.

WILLIAM DOUGLAS HOME.

THE CHILTERN HUNDREDS

First presented by Linnit & Dunfee Ltd., at the Theatre Royal, Brighton, on 18th August, 1947, and subsequently at the Vaudeville Theatre, London, on 26th August, 1947, with the following cast of characters :

(In the order of their appearance.)

THE EARL OF LISTER (Lord Lieutenant) . .	*A. E. Matthews*
THE COUNTESS OF LISTER (His Wife) .	*Marjorie Fielding*
JUNE FARRELL (of the American Embassy) . .	*Leora Dana*
BESSIE	*Diane Hart*
BEECHAM	*Michael Shepley*
LORD PYM (Lord Lister's Son)	*Peter Coke*
LADY CAROLINE SMITH (Lord Lister's Sister) .	*Edith Savile*
MR. CLEGHORN	*Tom Macaulay*

Directed by Colin Chandler

――――

SYNOPSIS OF SCENERY

SCENE : The Sitting-room of Lister Castle.   Summer, 1945.

ACT I

SCENE 1 . . General Election Result Day.   Lunch Time.
SCENE 2 . . . . The next morning.   Breakfast Time.

ACT II

SCENE 1 Saturday evening, the following week-end.   After Dinner.
SCENE 2 The By-Election.   Nomination Day.   Breakfast Time.

ACT III

SCENE 1 The By-Election Result Day.   A fortnight later.   Lunch Time.
SCENE 2 . . . . The same evening.   After Dinner.

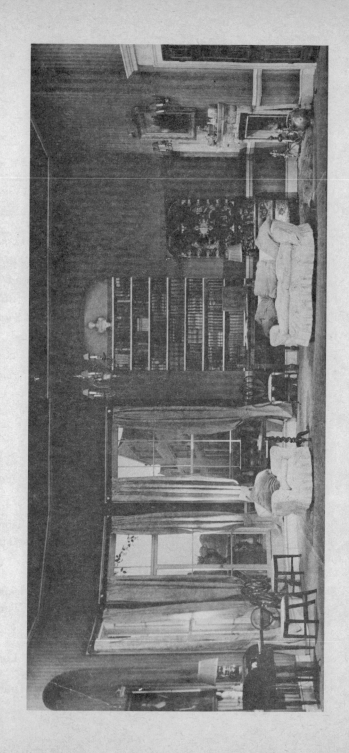

THE CHILTERN HUNDREDS

ACT I

Scene 1

Scene.—*The Sitting-room of Lister Castle.*

Time.—*Summer, 1945.*

There is a large bow window up R. *which looks on to the garden. A door down* L. *leads to other parts of the house. Up* L. *a cupboard, built into the wall. Up* C. *a large bookcase, and below it a table on which are a radio and various magazines. There is a sofa* L.C., *with an armchair to match* R.C. L. *of the armchair an occasional table. A desk* R., *with telephone. The fireplace is in the* L. *wall.*

It is lunch time on the day of the General Election result. LADY LISTER *is seated at the desk* R. *finishing a letter.* JUNE FARRELL, *wearing shorts and sandals, lies full length on the sofa, fast asleep.* LORD LISTER *is in the armchair* R.C., *reading a book on sport and absent-mindedly filling his pipe. From time to time he surveys the garden, which is somewhat overgrown with grass and weeds. A small rook rifle stands against the* L. *arm of his chair.*

LADY LISTER (*about to read from the letter*). What do you think of this, Joe ?

LORD LISTER. Excellent, my dear. First class.

LADY LISTER. Joe ! (*She looks round at him, then casts her eyes towards the sofa.*) Just look at June. June, dear, I really think you might have gone with Tony. After all, you are engaged.

LORD LISTER. This fellow says, " rabbits are most fond of those shrubs which grow within their reach." Dashed interesting.

LADY LISTER. I don't suppose the poor things know how nice the others taste. (*She sees the mess on the floor, and rises.*) I wish you'd keep your tobacco inside your pipe, Joe. (*Crossing above the armchair to the cupboard up* L.) I saw a fox down by the stables after breakfast, dear. (*She gets dustpan and brush from the cupboard.*)

LORD LISTER. Why the devil didn't you tell me before ?

LADY LISTER (*crossing* R. *again*). We've had so much to think about—and anyway it ran away when June went down to bathe. (*She sweeps up the bits* R. *of his chair.*)

LORD LISTER. Don't blame it. I'd run away if I saw a dashed Red Indian popping out of the water right under my nose, when I expected a duck.

7

LADY LISTER. Joe, you mustn't talk like that. It's so rude—
even in fun. (*She sweeps* L. *of his chair.*) After all, America wasn't
all Indians. Surely after the War of Independence there must have
been some white people settled there. You ought to know—you
went to Eton, Joe.

JUNE (*from the depth of the cushions*). Say, is it really true they
won old Waterloo around the campus there ?

LADY LISTER. I meant it, June. I think you should have gone
with Tony, June. (*She crosses to the cupboard for a duster and puts
away the dustpan and brush.*)

JUNE. I know. I heard you.

LADY LISTER. It would have given him moral support.

JUNE. Oh, hell. I couldn't go and watch a walk-over like this.
I want to see a fight.

LADY LISTER. I always used to go with Joe and hear the " count."

LORD LISTER. As far as I remember, dear—you used to wear a
skirt.

LADY LISTER (*moving to the sofa*). But still, the spirit's just the
same. (*Crossing to the window.*) Besides, she's got such very
pretty legs. (*She dusts.*)

LORD LISTER (*rising and moving to* R. *of sofa*). You wouldn't have
dressed like that if my father had been alive—pretty legs or no
pretty legs. Would have tickled you up with a riding crop, and the
prettier your legs the more he would have tickled you up. (*He
returns to the armchair and sits.*)

JUNE. I read about a guy like him at college once.

LADY LISTER (*who has moved down and picked up the rifle*). If
your father had been alive, Joe, I don't suppose you'd have kept a
rifle in the sitting-room. (*She crosses to his* R. *with the rifle.*)

LORD LISTER. Got to, my dear girl. In self-defence. (*To* LADY
LISTER, *who is dusting his rifle.*) Be careful, Molly, or you'll knock
the sight. (*To* JUNE.) My dear girl, my father had eighteen
gardeners, ten footmen, and six keepers here. Forked out a thousand
a year to keep the rabbits off the borders. Now, after three damn
wars, I've got no gardener—one gamekeeper who is an ex-conscien-
tious objector and faints when he sees a rabbit in a snare——

LADY LISTER. You've still got Beecham, dear. (*She replaces the
rifle and dusts the table beside him.*)

LORD LISTER. That damn fellow !

JUNE. I love Beecham, he's just swell. He's England, Joe.

LORD LISTER. He may be England, but he's damned expensive.

LADY LISTER. You're most unfair to Beecham, Joe. When he
came here in 1920, we engaged him as a footman. There was nothing
to suggest he would have to guard the herbaceous border in his spare
time—as a sort of scarecrow and retriever mixed. (*She is on her
knees, dusting the legs of the table.*)

LORD LISTER. Moll, I wish you'd stop fiddling about.

LADY LISTER. Well, someone's got to do the dusting, dear.

JUNE. I did it before breakfast, Moll.

LADY LISTER (*rising*). You might have told me, June.

LORD LISTER. It's dashed well time we got a maid.

LADY LISTER (*crossing to the desk and putting down the duster*). We've got one, Joe. At last. I do hope Tony's won. (*She crosses to the radio table, puts on her glasses and picks up the* Radio Times.) It should be through by lunch time, shouldn't it ?

LORD LISTER. It isn't only rabbits in the garden now. Dashed foxes, too.

JUNE (*sitting up*). Say, you can't wait ! You just can't wait to hear the news !

LORD LISTER. I take no part in Party Politics. I haven't done for twenty years. (*He rises, crosses and sits* L. *of* JUNE *on the sofa.*)

JUNE. But, Joe, he's your son !

LORD LISTER. The Labour fellow's someone's son as well. He's very sound I'd say.

LADY LISTER. I hope so—I voted for him.

JUNE. Say ! Say, what is this ? Joe, YOU didn't vote against your only son ?

LORD LISTER. I haven't got a vote. In England we disfranchise lunatics and peers.

JUNE. Not peeresses ?

(LADY LISTER *laughs*.)

LORD LISTER. Not under the second heading, anyway. It's up to the Medical Authorities to decide whether some of 'em come under the first.

JUNE. What makes Tony stand Conservative if you're both like this ?

LADY LISTER. Oh, Tony's very young. He's got lots of time to learn.

JUNE. Say, don't you realise what's happening to-day ? Tony, your son and heir, is fighting an Election that's been won since Cromwell's time by the eldest son of the family.

LADY LISTER. That's right, dear. I explained that to you when you came here first.

JUNE. Well, gee, it's NEWS. It gets right back behind your skin. It's like the Coronation.

LORD LISTER. Better weather—far. I had to walk from Westminster to Dover Street in all my robes. Couldn't get a taxi anywhere.

LADY LISTER. You should have gone by underground.

LORD LISTER. I didn't dare. Afraid I'd catch my ermine in the moving stairs.

LADY LISTER (*putting down the* Radio Times). What will Tony do if he gets beaten, Joe ?

LORD LISTER. He won't get beaten, Moll. This Seat's been Tory ever since Queen Anne.

LADY LISTER. Joe, Queen Anne's dead. (*She turns on the radio.*)

LORD LISTER. The Tories aren't, round here. They never die.

LADY LISTER. But Tory doesn't mean a thing. (*The voice of the* ANNOUNCER *begins to come through*.) They vote for something just because they like its face. That's exactly why I wanted June to go to-day.

LORD LISTER. It's too late now, my dear. They voted weeks ago.

RADIO ANNOUNCER. . . . and the Opposition parties hold a hundred seats. Here is the state of parties up to twelve o'clock this morning. Conservatives twenty-two, Nationals one, Liberal Nationals one, Labour ninety-nine, Independent one. The party gains and losses are as follows :—Conservative gains one, losses forty-five ; Labour gains forty-eight, losses none ; Liberal gains none, losses twó.

LADY LISTER. You see ! There's going to be a change. I knew it, Joe. How horrid people are. (*She switches off the radio*.) I can't listen any more. Poor Mrs. Churchill ! He's ringing up in any case.

JUNE. P'raps Mrs. Churchill voted Labour, Moll.

LADY LISTER. She couldn't have.

JUNE. Well, you did, dear.

LADY LISTER. I know, but I've been Labour all along. (*She crosses to the desk and sits*.) Now listen, Joe—are these all right ? This is if Tony wins. (*Reading from a letter*.) ' Dear Mr. Cleghorn, As you know, my husband, being Lord Lieutenant of the County, takes no part in Party Politics.'

JUNE. Say, what's a Lord Lieutenant ?

LORD LISTER. Oh, a Gauleiter, my dear. Yes, yes—go on.

LADY LISTER. ' We therefore feel able to write and say how much we appreciate the spirit in which you fought the Election. And we hope that you will come and see us any time you care to call.' And this is if HE wins. ' Dear Mr. Cleghorn, As you know, my husband, etc., etc., etc. We feel able to write and congratulate you on your victory over our son, and we hope that you will come and spend a week-end with us so that we can get to know each other better. Yours sincerely, Molly Lister.'

LORD LISTER. Asking him to stay !

LADY LISTER. We must, Joe. You're Lord Lieutenant.

LORD LISTER. But—dash it all—he called me a parasite !

LADY LISTER. What nonsense, dear.

LORD LISTER. He did, my dear. It's in the *Advertiser*. (*He rises to get it from the table up* R.C.) Here. Listen to this, by Jove. (*He reads from it*.) ' In a speech at Lister Market, Mr. James Cleghorn, the Labour Candidate, said : " I ask you, the Electors of East Milton, to vote for me, Jackie Cleghorn, the workers' candidate, the man who has slaved for thirty years beneath the heel of the plutocrat—— " '

LADY LISTER.   That's not ' parasite,' dear.   That's ' plutocrat.'
It's rather flattering—I wish that it was true.

LORD LISTER.   Listen, woman.   (*He continues reading.*)   —" and
NOT to vote for Viscount Pym, the young aristocrat from Lister
Castle, the boy who went from Eton and Oxford into the Household
Cavalry—the son of a million Listers—the heir to a thousand
capitalists—the last of a long, and alas, uninterrupted line of pluto-
crats and peers and parasites."   There you are.

LADY LISTER.   Yes, but he doesn't say, actually, you—Joe.

LORD LISTER.   Maybe.   (*He puts down the paper and crosses up* R.)
But he leaves it open.   Dashed open, I'd say.

LADY LISTER.   Besides, these politicians never say the things they
mean.   They put them straight in prison if they do.   And so they
never do.

LORD LISTER (*looking out of the window*).   It's there, Molly.   It's
there, by Jove.

LADY LISTER.   What, dear ?   That naughty fox ?

LORD LISTER.   Don't move.   Don't move an inch.   (*He moves
down for his rifle.*)   A huge buck rabbit !   (*He loads the rifle.*)   I've
got to get this infernal window open.

LADY LISTER (*rising*).   Joe, you must NOT fire that gun in here.

LORD LISTER.   Be quiet, my dear.

LADY LISTER (*crossing* C.).   I'm going out.   I cannot bear that
noise.

LORD LISTER.   You can't go out.   It'll see you through the
passage window.   Get inside the cupboard if it frightens you.   Go
on.   It won't sit feeding there all day.

(LADY LISTER *crosses up* L.   LORD LISTER *moves to the window.   The
telephone rings.*   LADY LISTER *makes a move towards the desk.*)

LADY LISTER.   It's Tony, Joe.   It's sure to be.

LORD LISTER.   Get back, Molly !   Get back !

LADY LISTER.   I should have thought the result of the election's
more important than a silly rabbit.

LORD LISTER.   Balderdash.   There'll be another one in five years'
time.

LADY LISTER.   All right—well, answer it yourself.   (*She goes
back to the cupboard.*)

LORD LISTER.   I can't.

(BESSIE *enters down* L.   *The telephone rings again—an intermittent
country ring.*)

Get out.   Send Beecham here at once.

(BESSIE *hurries out down* L.)

What am I to do, Molly ?   If I open the window, the telephone'll
frighten it.   Can I shoot it through the glass ?

LADY LISTER. Certainly not. There's quite enough bomb-damage unrepaired without you adding to it.

(BEECHAM *enters down* L.)

BEECHAM. You sent for me, my lord ?

(*The telephone rings again.*)

LORD LISTER. I did. That telephone. It's ringing. Hear it, eh ?

BEECHAM. I do, my lord.

LORD LISTER. Well, answer it.

BEECHAM. Very good, my lord. (*He shuts the door and starts to walk across.*)

LORD LISTER. Hi. Beecham, halt ! You cross that sky-line by the sofa and I'll sack you on the spot. Stoop, man, stoop.

(*The telephone rings again as* BEECHAM *crosses to the desk, stooping.*)

And sit down when you get there.

(BEECHAM *sits on the chair at the desk and answers the telephone.*)

BEECHAM. Hullo . . . Yes—this is Lister Castle—yes.

LORD LISTER. And keep down, man.

BEECHAM (*bobbing*). His Lordship's Agent. Yes, Mr. Brown . . . No. His lordship and her ladyship are both—are both out shooting in the grounds.

LORD LISTER. Don't chatter, Beecham. Cut it short.

BEECHAM. I'll take a message, certainly . . . I see. Two thousand. Thank you, sir . . . He started back some time ago ? I thank you, sir. (*He hangs up.*) His lordship's Agent on the line, my lord.

LORD LISTER I gathered that. Now pack it in.

LADY LISTER. What happened, Beecham ? Did he win ?

BEECHAM. Master Tony lost, my lady. By two thousand votes.

JUNE (*jumping up*). He couldn't have. The little sap !

LORD LISTER (*at boiling point*). JUNE !

JUNE (*subsiding on to the sofa again*). O.K., Joe. Sorry. Let it have the works.

BEECHAM (*as* LORD LISTER *is at last about to open the window*). It's terrible, my lord.

LORD LISTER. What's terrible ? The people like a change. Relax.

BEECHAM. This seat's been won from Lister Castle by the Tories for two hundred years, my lord.

LORD LISTER (*losing patience*). Beecham ! You come in here and sit about discussing politics as though you owned the place. Shut up. Will you—SHUT UP ! (*Dangerously calm.*) I'm opening the window now. (*To* BEECHAM.) If anybody talks again —take their name.

(LADY LISTER *disappears into the cupboard. For the first time there is silence. He opens the window, raises his rifle, takes aim. The loud fluctuating note of a motor horn is heard ; tyres swish over the gravel ; brakes squeal ; a door slams.*)

Damnation ! Hell and blast ! He's frightened it. (*He slams the window shut.*)

JUNE (*rising and crossing up* R.). Joe—take the shell out, Joe.

LORD LISTER. I'll never get another chance like that. (*He unloads, and stands the rifle up by the window.*)

BEECHAM. May I get up, my lord ?

LORD LISTER. That's up to you. Depends on how you feel. (*He moves down to the desk.*)

BEECHAM (*rising painfully*). I thought perhaps the creature might be contemplating further nourishment, my lord.

LORD LISTER. What ! Nourishment ! My foot ! Would you be keen on feeding if a screaming Yankee horn like that went off when you were having lunch ?

BEECHAM. It often has, my lord. On occasions I have suffered indigestion—but invariably I return to finish what is left upon my plate.

(TONY *enters down* L.)

TONY. I say, what's happened ? Beecham feeling faint ?

LORD LISTER. Dash it, Tony, can't you drive a car more like a gentleman ?

JUNE. Hell, Tony, how'd you lose ?

TONY. Because the other fellow got more votes.

JUNE. I guess he must have done.

TONY. Where's mother ?

LORD LISTER (*crossing to the cupboard up* L.). Oh, my God ! Molly, you can come out now.

LADY LISTER (*appearing*). Is it all over ? It's very hot in there —like a Turkish Bath. (*She sees* TONY.) Poor Tony. I'm so sorry.

JUNE. Well ! You voted Labour, what do you expect ?

LADY LISTER (*up* R.C.). Yes, yes. I know I did. I backed the losing side. I always do. But now they've won, they've lost my sympathy.

(BEECHAM *crosses* L.)

TONY (*below the sofa*). A bit late then. I say, I'm hoarse. Hey, Beecham, what about a drink ?

BEECHAM. I'll fetch the sherry in, my lord.

TONY. I had to make a speech and tell old Cleghorn what a decent chap he was. And so he is.

LADY LISTER (*to* BEECHAM, *who is standing at the door*). What's the matter, Beecham ?

BEECHAM (*to* TONY). May I say how mortified I am to hear of your defeat, my lord.

TONY. Oh, thanks. Oh, thanks a lot.

BEECHAM. I dare not contemplate what the Tenth Earl, your grandfather, would have remarked on this unhappy day, my lord.

LORD LISTER (*coming down between the sofa and the armchair and crossing to the door*). I'll tell you what he would have remarked, Beecham. Just what I'm remarking now. ' Get out and fetch those something something drinks.'

BEECHAM. Er—very good, my lord.

(*He goes out down* L.)

LORD LISTER. Damned ninny ! Crying over spilt milk. I'm going to wash.

(*He goes out, leaving the door open.*)

LADY LISTER (*crossing to the door*). Yes, come along. I'm sorry, Tony dear. And if it wasn't for the rabbit, your father would be sorry too.

(*She exits down* L., *shutting the door after her.*)

JUNE. Oh, hell, I think you stink. Old Beecham could have won this dump.

TONY. If he'd had you to help him, eh ?

JUNE. I guess so. Yeah.

TONY. Of course, you know so much about our politics.

JUNE (*moving* C. *towards him*). Well, tell me some.

TONY. It isn't me that stinks. The Tory party stinks.

JUNE. It's a bad workman who complains of his tools.

TONY. It's a silly fool who tries to win a seat from Lister Castle in a modern world. Of course, you wouldn't understand. Americans are snobs. They bite a fellow's ear off if he has a coronet. That doesn't happen here.

JUNE. I guess it might. (*She bites his ear, playfully.*) I guess they twist his tail instead. Poor little man. (*She kisses him.*) Just go on trying.

TONY. I'm damned if I'll try again. I've had the Tories.

JUNE. What's the next move, then ?

TONY. Oh, chivvy rabbits round for Dad. Or nip around the house for Mother, dusting things and sweeping up the crumbs. (*He sits on the sofa,* L. *end.*)

JUNE (R. *of the sofa*). Say, aren't you just ambitious ! What's our Bessie for ?

TONY. I dunno. I was wondering last night. In bed, you know. I couldn't sleep before the Count. Old Bessie kind of crossed my mind, that's all.

(BEECHAM *enters with the sherry, closing the door after him.*)

(*To* BEECHAM.) I say, what's Bessie do ?

BEECHAM. In what respect. my lord ? (*He moves to the table above the sofa.*)

TONY. About the house.

BEECHAM (*relieved*). She does the rooms, my lord. The usual routine housemaid's work—assisted by her ladyship, of course. (*He places the sherry on the table.*)

JUNE. She's parlourmaid and kitchenmaid and housemaid all rolled into one ?

BEECHAM. Precisely, miss.

TONY. Oh, damn. That's closed an avenue.

BEECHAM (*pouring out two glasses of sherry*). Have you found Bessie wanting then, my lord, in some respect ?

TONY. Oh, no. Oh, rather not. What should she want ?

BEECHAM. I find if difficult to say, my lord.

JUNE (*watching him closely*). She's pretty, Beecham, isn't she ?

BEECHAM. Yes, miss. I will concede she has a certain rustic charm. (*He moves towards her, with two glasses of sherry on a tray.*)

JUNE. Say, Beecham, do you ever bounce her on your knee ?

BEECHAM. Some sherry, miss ? (*She takes it.*) For you, my lord ?

TONY (*taking it*). Oh, thanks. Did Bessie vote for me ?

BEECHAM. I couldn't say, my lord. I doubt it, though. She's Commonwealth. (*He returns and replaces the tray on the table.*)

JUNE. What's that ?

BEECHAM (*considering*). Well, miss—a nervous spinster's version of a Communist might meet the case.

TONY. Good show. I'll drink her health.

(BEECHAM *crosses down* L.)

To Bessie -- What's her name ?

BEECHAM (*disapproving strongly*). Miss Sykes, my lord. (*He opens the door.*)

TONY. To Bessie Sykes ! Escaped from Toryism and the shackles of Conservative Decay. (*He lifts his glass and drinks.*)

BEECHAM. You seem to take defeat with fortitude, my lord.

TONY. I do. Why not ?

BEECHAM. Provided your reaction's prompted by your native grit—and not by irresponsibility—I have no axe to grind, my lord.

(*He exits down* L.)

TONY. I suppose he thinks I ought to cry a bit ?

JUNE. I'm glad there's someone here who understands what's happened to the family.

TONY. June, dash it ! Not you too ! Come and kiss me, please.

(*She does, sitting* R. *of him on the sofa.* LORD LISTER *enters down* L.)

LORD LISTER. Dashed close thing, Tony, eh ?

TONY. Two thousand odd.

LORD LISTER. I had my finger on the trigger as you blew the horn.

(*Enter* LADY LISTER.)

JUNE. I'm telling Tony he's got to find a job.

LADY LISTER (*crossing* R. *to the desk*). I've got a job for Tony. I want a run made of wire netting for my ducks. (*She seals the two letters.*)

(JUNE *rises, puts her empty glass on the drink table and crosses to the window.*)

LORD LISTER (*at the drink table*). Well, that's alright. There's always something to be done if one can only find it and someone hasn't done it first. (*He pours himself a glass of sherry.*)

LADY LISTER. I've asked the Labour man to stay this week-end, dear.

TONY. Oh, jolly decent of you.

LADY LISTER. Oh, and, Joe—your sister Caroline.

LORD LISTER. What for? She bores me blue. (*He moves up towards the window.*)

LADY LISTER. Well, you won't have to talk to Mr. Cleghorn all the time.

JUNE (*in* LORD LISTER'S *ear*). There's a bunny eating your begonias.

LORD LISTER. What? What?

JUNE. A bunny—eating—your——

LORD LISTER. What! Dash the thing, Beecham was right. (*He puts his glass on the table up* R.C. *and picks up the rifle.*) Stand still.

(BEECHAM *enters.*)

BEECHAM. Luncheon is——

LORD LISTER. Shut up.

LADY LISTER. I think his lordship is preparing dinner, Beecham.

(LORD LISTER *has opened the window and is taking aim. He fires.*)

LORD LISTER. After it, Beecham. Quick!

(BEECHAM *goes out of the window at the double.*)

Don't worry about the Election, Tony. It's just the swing of the pendulum. Take Charles the First and Cromwell. Different types —that's all. (*Shouting through the window.*) Hey! Not there, you fool. By the box bush. That's it. Pick it up. It's not a tiger, man.

LADY LISTER. Joe, what are you going to do with Tony?

LORD LISTER (*with an eye on operations outside*). Oh, go back to the Army. Go into the Church. (*The rabbit has been retrieved ; he turns back to the room.*) All sorts of things to do. (*He stands the rifle by the window, picks up his sherry, and crosses* L. *above the sofa.*) I knew a fellow once, became a bookie. He lost thirty thousand quid in seven weeks. Oh, lots of things to do.

(BEECHAM *enters through the window, carrying a dead rabbit, and crosses below the sofa to the door.*)

BEECHAM (*at the door*). Luncheon is served, my lady.

LADY LISTER. Thank you, Beecham. Come along, June.

(*She crosses* L. *with two letters from the desk, followed by* JUNE. BEECHAM *is holding the door open for them.* TONY *puts his glass on the table behind the sofa and rises.*)

(*To* BEECHAM.) Oh, will you post these, please ? No, just the one with M.P. on the end. (*She tears the other up.*)

(LADY LISTER *and* JUNE *go out down* L. TONY *and* LORD LISTER *move to follow them,* LORD LISTER *putting his glass on the table above the sofa.*)

TONY (*as he passes the rabbit*). Not a very big one, is it, Dad ?

LORD LISTER. Too many of 'em here. We'll never get 'em down if we don't fight 'em back. We must fight back.

(TONY *and* LORD LISTER *have disappeared.* BEECHAM *starts to clear the tray at the table above the sofa. The telephone rings. He goes to answer it, rabbit in hand.*)

BEECHAM. Hullo ? Lister Castle . . . Yes, the *Advertiser* ? . . . His lordship's reaction. Lord Pym's do you mean ? . . . No, quite, you heard his speech . . . The Earl himself ? Lord Lister is at lunch just now, but I can let you have his views. As Lord Lieutenant, Lord Lister is neutral, taking no part in Party Politics. As a man, and a Pym, his lordship feels the situation most acutely. The effect on the human organism of two hundred years' tradition overthrown since one o'clock is hard to gauge at first. All we can say is that the mind is numbed, while kindly nature breathes her healing balm around her stricken child . . . A statement ? No, I cannot possibly disturb the Earl at lunch. One moment. (*He thinks for a moment and remembers.*) You may quote his lordship as saying—shortly after the result was declared—" We must fight back." Yes, that is it. (*He repeats it, in a voice vibrant with emotion.*) WE MUST FIGHT BACK.

(*He hangs up the receiver and crosses to collect the sherry tray. Then, tray in one hand and rabbit in the other—leaves the room.*)

CURTAIN

ACT I

SCENE 2

The following morning.

There is a round table C., *laid ready for breakfast. The sofa has been pushed back up* L., *and the armchair up* R.C. *A wheeled trolley stands* L.C. *(See Furniture and Property Plot.)*

BESSIE, *obviously behindhand, is laying the last two places. As she finishes she picks up the silver basket and makes for the door down* L., *meeting* BEECHAM *bringing in the coffee. She goes out.*

BEECHAM *crosses to the table and puts down the coffee. He crosses to the trolley, takes the morning papers from the middle shelf and places them on the radio table up* L.C. *Retaining* The Times *for himself, he comes down* C. *and, with varying expressions on his face, starts to look through it for the articles devoted to the Election results.*

LORD LISTER *enters through the French windows, carrying a rabbit snare. He comes down to* R. *of* BEECHAM.

LORD LISTER. Is breakfast ready yet?

BEECHAM. It is, my lord.

LORD LISTER. About time too. *(Holding up the snare.)* I found this in the potting shed. A rabbit snare. Dashed useful things. *(He puts it beside his plate.)* The bath water was cold to-day.

BEECHAM. I'm sorry to hear that, my lord.

LORD LISTER. It's not your sympathy I want. *(He takes the paper from* BEECHAM.) However sorry you may be, that doesn't heat the bath water. The fire must be kept in—at night. That's all one asks. It isn't much to ask. Who's job is it?

BEECHAM *(crossing to the trolley)*. It should be the odd-man's, my lord—but as we don't employ one—the responsibility devolves on me, my lord. *(He lifts the lid of the dish for* LORD LISTER, *who has come to the trolley.)*

LORD LISTER. Well, why the devil was the water cold? *(He helps himself to a duck's egg.)*

BEECHAM. I'm afraid the boiler slipped my mind last night, my lord. The day's events had served to drive domestic details of that nature from my head.

LORD LISTER *(crossing to the table)*. What day's events? What happened yesterday? *(He sits* L. *of the table and commences his breakfast.)*

BEECHAM. According to the papers, the Electorate conspired to bring the Socialists to power, my lord.

LORD LISTER. Oh, that! Well—what the devil's that to do with you?

BEECHAM. I feel the matter very strongly, as I told your lordship yesterday.

18

LORD LISTER. Daresay you do. That's no excuse for going round and sabotaging everything. That's anarchy, by Jove.

BEECHAM. I did it unintentionally, my lord. I felt so low last night, I took a sleeping draught and went to bed at nine. (*He crosses to above the table.*)

LORD LISTER. What sort of sleeping draught ?

BEECHAM. Three Veganin, washed down with port, my lord.

LORD LISTER. Now look here, Beecham. Pull yourself together —and get this in your head. The Labour Party's IN, and nothing you can do or say can get 'em out again.

BEECHAM. A counsel of despair, my lord. (*He pours coffee.*)

LORD LISTER. It's common sense. So stop sulking. Why— damn it—anyone would think you were Winston from the shindy you're kicking up.

BEECHAM. I can't help taking Master Tony's failure as a personal affront, my lord. After all your lordship has done for the County, I regard it as the height of ingratitude to spurn your son in favour of a man without tradition—or refinement—or one single link with those who made this country what it is. I mean, of course, the British aristocracy, my lord.

LORD LISTER. Oh, poppycock ! We've been found out, that's all. (*He takes sugar.*)

BEECHAM. I can't agree, my lord. I regard yesterday's poll as a direct result of the sinister influence emanating from those countries now in the grip of social revolution. I refer, of course, to——

LORD LISTER. Anyway, I bet old Stalin's bath water is hot.

BEECHAM. That may be so, my lord. But—if it is—the reason is not far to seek. The servants in the Kremlin doubtless fear the axe.

LORD LISTER. Exactly. There's a lot of good in Communism— if one takes a thoroughly unbiased view.

BEECHAM. I cannot agree, my lord.

LORD LISTER. I don't expect you to.

BEECHAM. Whatever your lordship may say, I regard the future with profound distrust. If I may crave——

LORD LISTER (*who has been trying to read the paper for some time*). Beecham ! How the devil can I read the cricket scores if you keep chattering ? One more word about politics—just ONE more, mark you—and I'll send you off to Blackpool for a month.

(BEECHAM, *discouraged and silenced, fiddles round the table and picks up the snare.*)

BEECHAM. Will I place this in the gun-room, then, my lord ?

LORD LISTER. No. You will not. You'll place it in the border —by the box bush—where I shot the rabbit yesterday.

BEECHAM. Yes—very good, my lord.

LORD LISTER. It works like this. You stick the wooden peg straight into the ground. Like this. (*He stuffs it through the loaf.*)

You bend the wire like this. And then the noose hangs down—just right—and pretty near the ground. You see ?

BEECHAM. I do, my lord.

LORD LISTER. And then the rabbit comes along like this. On it's run, you see ? It doesn't see the wire, and pops its head right through—like this.

(*The final graphic gesture ensnares his wrist.* BEECHAM *is in the act of releasing him when* LADY LISTER *enters down* L.)

LADY LISTER. Joe ! What are you doing, Joe ? (*She crosses to* R. *of the table and sits. She has cereal for breakfast.*)

BEECHAM. Excuse me, my lord.

LORD LISTER. It's all right, Moll, don't fuss. I'm getting Beecham's mind off politics. (*To* BEECHAM.) Now take it out and set it. Keep your feet out of the bed—and let it clear the ground by just an inch.

BEECHAM. Yes—very good, my lord.

(BEECHAM *goes out into the garden.*)

LORD LISTER. Poor devil'll go crackers if he doesn't get a hobby. Goes on harping on the General Election. If we don't watch it, he'll get to be as big a bore as Gladstone was. The bath water was cold, my dear.

LADY LISTER (*counter-attacking*). I know. Perhaps that's why you haven't made your bed this morning, dear.

LORD LISTER (*routed*). Oh, sorry—I forgot.

LADY LISTER. It doesn't matter actually. (*She has been looking through her letters.*) The laundry's coming, so we must change the sheets. Still, you mustn't let things slide.

LORD LISTER (*stung*). What's that ?

LADY LISTER. I said you mustn't let things slide. Dear Joe, I know exactly how you feel. But, dear, the Labour Party's IN and nothing you can do or say can get 'em out again.

LORD LISTER. Well, I'll be damned !

(BEECHAM *enters through the french window, wiping soil off his hands.*)

BEECHAM. The gin is in position now, my lord. (*He crosses down* L.)

LORD LISTER. Oh, right.

LADY LISTER. So stop worrying about the Election, or else I'll have to send you off to stay with Caroline.

(LORD LISTER *looks awkward.* BEECHAM *goes out down* L. *with a sardonic smile on his face.*)

LORD LISTER. I'd rather shoot myself than stay with Caroline.

LADY LISTER. What nonsense, dear. She's your own flesh and blood.

LORD LISTER. In spite of that, she looks exactly like a horse.

LADY LISTER. Now, don't be catty, dear.

LORD LISTER. I'm talking about horses, Moll.

LADY LISTER. I've got a letter from her here. (*Reading.*) ' Dearest Molly,—How too, too terrible ! You poor dears ! My heart goes out to you and Joe in your unhappiness—— '

LORD LISTER. What the devil is she nattering about now ?

LADY LISTER. The Election, dear. (*Reading on.*) ' I've just heard the wireless. How hateful people are. After all poor dear Mr. Churchill has done for them—— '

LORD LISTER. I like that ! She loathed old Churchill's guts before the war.

LADY LISTER. Please don't keep interrupting, dear. It's very difficult to read. (*She reads on.*) ' They turn against him now, and spurn him like a stranger cur—— ' (*puzzled*) then in brackets— ' Julius Caesar.' What does she mean, dear ?

LORD LISTER. Dashed if I know.

(TONY *comes in down* L. *in battle dress—M.C. ribbon and Africa Star—looking very smart and rather hurried.*)

TONY. Morning, Mother. Morning, Father.

LADY LISTER. Tony dear—what's a stranger cur ?

TONY. Dashed if I know. (*At the trolley, helping himself to an egg.*) I suppose—a cur that's stranger than another cur.

LADY LISTER (*to* TONY). This is from Aunt Caroline. (*She reads on.*) ' Thanks for asking me for next week-end. I don't want to come—— '

LORD LISTER. Good.

LADY LISTER. ' —— but I will—— '

LORD LISTER Damn.

LADY LISTER. ' ——to help you, you poor darling—— '

LORD LISTER. I shall go to Blackpool.

LADY LISTER. Why Blackpool, dear ?

LORD LISTER. Well, Brighton—Bognor Regis—anywhere.

LADY LISTER. You won't, my dear ; you asked her here.

LORD LISTER. Me ? Never in a thousand years.

(TONY *has brought his egg to his place at the breakfast table, then fetched a paper from the table upstage. He now moves down to above* LADY LISTER *and, during the following, kisses her, then sits and begins his brekfast.*)

LADY LISTER (*reading on*). ' I suppose that dreadful, vulgar—— ' (*As* TONY *kisses her.*) Good morning, dear. ' ——self-made Mr. Cleghorn will be there. Why MUST Joe ask a mountebank like that to stay at Lister ? If poor dear father were alive I'm sure he would turn in his grave—— '

LORD LISTER. He couldn't, dear—he was cremated !

LADY LISTER (*reading on*). ' Give poor dear gallant Anthony my love and kisses—— '

TONY. UGH!

LADY LISTER (*ignoring him*). 'Tell him I am grateful to him for saving me from Hitler, even if East Milton is not——'

LORD LISTER. What on earth would Hitler want with Caroline?

LADY LISTER (*sailing on*). 'Oh, noble Anthony!' (*Puzzled again.*) 'J. Caesar'—in brackets again.

LORD LISTER. Why the devil does she keep harping on that fellow Caesar?

LADY LISTER. I don't know, dear.

LORD LISTER. What the blazes has Caesar got to do with East Milton?

LADY LISTER. I still don't know, dear. It's almost finished now. (*She reads on.*) 'Your ever loving Caroline. P.S.—And what's poor Tony going to *do*?' Twice underlined. Tony dear—what *are* you going to do?

TONY. I'm going to the Depot to report.

LADY LISTER. And then?

TONY. I'm going to ask the Adjutant for week-end leave.

LORD LISTER. What? Why walk into it?

(JUNE *enters hurriedly down* L.)

LADY LISTER. He wants to see Aunt Caroline again.

TONY. I don't. I want to talk to Cleghorn about politics.

JUNE (*helping herself at the trolley*). Why talk to him?

TONY (*awkward at finding her there*). Oh, I dunno. I always like to learn the other fellow's point of view.

LADY LISTER. Good morning, June. (*She pours coffee for herself and* TONY.)

JUNE (*between* TONY *and* LADY LISTER). Good morning, Moll. Good morning, Joe.

LORD LISTER. What's that?

JUNE. I said, 'Good morning, Joe.'

LORD LISTER. Ah, yes. I've set a snare.

JUNE. You have? What for?

LORD LISTER. Oh—rabbits chiefly. It's a rabbit snare, you know.

LADY LISTER. Joe, do stop talking about rabbits!

LORD LISTER (*hurt*). Why? They interest me.

LADY LISTER. Yes, dear. I'm slowly learning that. So long as you've your beastly rabbits, you don't mind if Tony starves.

(TONY *looks up, his mouth full of egg.* JUNE *pours coffee.*)

LORD LISTER. What? Tony hungry? Have another piece of toast? (*He shoves the rack across.*) You're worse than Beecham, Moll. You ought to take a sedative.

LADY LISTER (*rising and crossing* L.C. *below the table*). I sometimes wonder if I didn't take one when I married you.

(LORD LISTER *winces.*)

I'm sorry, Joe. (*She goes to him.*) I'm worried about Tony's future—but it doesn't matter. Will you be a dear—and run along and make the breakfast for my ducks? It's in the scullery. I've got to go and do the laundry—they're coming here to-day. Oh—and, Joe, poor Clara's not been laying at all well, so give her more than all the others, dear. (*She crosses down* L.)

LORD LISTER (*mollified*). Yes—rather—yes. (*He rises.*) Yes—rather—yes. (*He crosses down* L.) Poor old Clara—of course I will.

(LADY LISTER *has gone out down* L. LORD LISTER *follows.*)

TONY. Why's everybody on the hop to-day?

JUNE. Reaction. Say, what time's your train?

TONY. Nine fifty-five. It only takes four minutes in the car.

JUNE. I'll run you down. You packed?

TONY. Old Beecham's up there now.

JUNE. O.K. I'll finish this and get the car. I'm sorry you're going.

TONY. I'll have leave this week-end.

JUNE. That's swell. And then?

TONY. Oh, I dunno. Maybe I'll stay on in the army, till some foreign gentleman splits my atom—in World War Number Three.

JUNE. You can't do that.

TONY. Why not?

JUNE. Because you've got no cash.

TONY. They pay one in the Army, dear.

JUNE. How much?

TONY. Oh, I dunno. About a mess-bill's worth.

JUNE. Hell, Tony! This is 1945! You've got to roll your sleeves right up—and make a pile of dough.

TONY. What for?

JUNE. For me—I guess.

TONY. I thought you had a lot.

JUNE. You think I'm going to keep you, kid?

TONY. Well, no. I wouldn't put it just like that.

JUNE. How would you put it, then?

TONY. Well—dash it, June. Don't pin me down, old girl. What's the matter with you, June? You've never been like this before. You got engaged to me. You knew I hadn't any money then.

JUNE. It isn't only money that you need

TONY. Well, what's the matter, then?

JUNE. I guess you need some guts.

TONY. Here—damn it, that's not fair. I don't want to boast, but fellows in the Army thought I had my share. Oh, I know I got the M.C. 'cos I lost myself near Tripoli—and found myself behind the German lines. But still, they said I had a lot of leadership and—drive and—things.

JUNE (*rising*). Well, why not use them now ? (*She crosses to the table above the sofa for a cigarette.*)

TONY. Well, dash it. You're talking as though I'm the only Tory candidate that's lost his seat. There's hundreds did.

JUNE. I'm not complaining that you lost. You get my goat because you let it get you down.

TONY. I haven't let it get me down. I sang in my bath this morning. At least, I didn't have a bath, because the water's cold. I think I'm being jolly brave. I had to plug a policy that's out of date——

JUNE. You might have thought of that before.

TONY. I've not had time to think—since 1939—what with reading maps and kit inspections—taking sand out of one's hair.

JUNE. I guess you haven't got it all out yet. Say, can't you just forget the past—and look ahead ?

TONY. What at ?

JUNE. At life. At us. At you and me. At lots of yelling children with a father on the dole.

TONY. June, not at breakfast, please.

JUNE. Yes, kid. At breakfast—lunch and tea and dinner—every day and every night. A crowd of hungry little kids—all looking at you with reproachful eyes—and screaming for their ration books. You've got to face it, boy.

TONY (*shuddering*). I can't.

JUNE. You've got to WORK.

TONY. I'm not brought up to work. I'm culture—all the things you Yankees like—that's me ! The upper crust that makes the bread of life digestible ! The world needs men of leisure (*he puts his foot up on the armchair*) —more than ever—in these hectic days. And I was born to be a man of leisure. It's a sin for me to work. It's a betrayal of my birthright. It's——

JUNE (*moving towards him*). Say, listen, Tony—don't you want to work for—me ?

TONY. What ? No.

(*Her eyes blaze.*)

I mean—well, if I had to—yes.

JUNE (*going up to him*). I'm telling you—you have to.

TONY. But—to work for you—it's—it's—it's taking coals to Newcastle.

JUNE. I guess we needn't bring in Newcastle. (*She crosses up L.*) I'm telling you—if you don't get a job, you don't get me.

TONY. All right. Well, if you say so——

JUNE. Good. Then, what's it going to be ? (*She crosses to L. of him.*)

TONY. I'll stay on in the army, if you like.

JUNE. We've had that once—and I don't like.

TONY. Oh, have a heart. It's all that I can do. For five years

I've been taught to kill. I did it jolly well. But now—the killing's off. It's dashed bad luck. It leaves a fellow in the air.

JUNE. I'll say it does. (*She goes to the window.*)

TONY. June—have you got no sympathy ? It's all they trained me for.

JUNE. Well, why not start right in and train yourself for something else ?

TONY. Well—what ?

JUNE. Hell—anything. My father and my uncles—in the States. They only had a hundred dollars to their name when they were kids. Where are they now ? They're millionaires—and shall I tell you why ?

TONY. No, I can guess.

JUNE. Because they roughed it. And because they worked like blacks. And now—all three of them—are millionaires.

TONY. But I don't want to be a millionaire.

JUNE. I'd say you needn't worry about that. (*She crosses* C.) I'll be content if you can make enough to keep yourself in underpants.

TONY. I don't wear underpants.

JUNE. Say, listen, Tony—I'm dead serious.

TONY. I know you are.

JUNE. I'm telling you—if you don't get a job—then our engagement's off. You think that over at the Depot and then give me your decision next week-end. O.K. ?

TONY (*broken*). O.K.

JUNE. I'll go and get the car.

(JUNE *goes out—leaving* TONY *in the depths of depression, lighting a cigarette.* BESSIE *comes in to clear away the breakfast.*)

BESSIE. Oh, I'm sorry, sir. I thought you were finished.

TONY. So I am. You carry on. (*He gets up and crosses to the window with his coffee cup. After watching her for a moment.*) Er— Bessie, tell me something. How much do you get for doing this ?

BESSIE. Two pounds a week, my lord. (*She puts the papers on the armchair and then the cups and saucers on the tray.*)

TONY. Two—a week. Ah—yes, I see. That isn't very much. (*Pause.*) Do men get more than women for this sort of thing ?

BESSIE. Oh, yes, my lord. Men's stronger, see ?

TONY. Oh, are they ? Yes, I see. Er—tell me—is it very hard —this work ?

BESSIE. Oh, no, my lord.

TONY. When do you start ?

BESSIE. I'm always up at half-past five. (*She clears three large plates.*)

TONY. Good God !

BESSIE. And, usually, I'm through by——

TONY. Thank you, Bessie—that's enough.

BESSIE. I'm sorry, sir. (*She takes the tray to the trolley.*)

TONY. No, not a bit. If you were married, would you mind your husband not having a job ?

BESSIE. Not if I loved him, no, my lord. I'd work my fingers to the bone for him. (*She crosses to* L. *of table for the bread.*)

TONY. You would ?

BESSIE. Oh, yes—my lord. It's only them with too much money who gets martyrs to it, sir. (*She crosses to the trolley with the bread.*)

TONY. I so agree.

BESSIE (*coming to the table again*). My mother always says, ' Poor peoples' happier than rich.'

TONY. She does ? Well, why is that ?

BESSIE. Because they have to do with all the things that don't need money to be got. And them's the best things in the end.

TONY. Such as ?

BESSIE. You can't buy 'appiness, my lord.

TONY (*moving towards her*). By jove—that's true.

BESSIE. Nor love, my lord.

TONY (*moving nearer still*). Nor love—by jove.

BESSIE (*embarrassed*). I'm talking out of turn, my lord. (*She crosses to the trolley with* LADY LISTER'S *cereal plate.*)

TONY. No, rather not. I like talking to you, Bessie. Er—tell me, you're Commonwealth, they say.

BESSIE. That's right. I follow Mum.

(LORD LISTER *enters down* L., *with a plate of duck food in one hand and a highly-coloured book in the other.*)

TONY. Oh, yes. And Mum, I take it, is a bit left wing.

BESSIE. I'm sure I couldn't say, my lord.

LORD LISTER (*who has crossed to the table*). Dashed good book in the scullery. " She Never Knew What Hit Her." Wonder whose it is ? (*He sits at his place at the table.*)

BESSIE. It's mine, my lord.

LORD LISTER. Oh, really—finished with it ?

BESSIE. Yes, my lord.

LORD LISTER. Oh, good—I'll loan it from you if I may.

(BEECHAM *enters down* L. *He holds the door open for* JUNE, *who follows him in.*)

JUNE. Come on. You'll miss your train.

BEECHAM (*at the door*). Her ladyship is coming down to say ' good-bye,' my lord. She's in the linen cupboard.

TONY. Good. (*Crossing to the trolley to put down his cup.*) I'll come along.

BESSIE. Safe trip, my lord. (*She crosses down* C.)

TONY. Oh, thanks. I hope we meet again this next week-end.

(BESSIE *blushes.* JUNE *and* BEECHAM *react unfavourably.*)

I'm just off, Dad.

(*He exits down* L., *followed by* JUNE *and* BEECHAM. *They leave the door open.*)

LORD LISTER. Eh ? What ? Oh, yes, well come back soon.

(BESSIE *gives a sob.*)

(*Rising.*) I say—I say, don't do that. (*He comes to her.*) No need to worry—he's only going to Aldershot.

(*He goes out down* L. *with the plate of duck food and book.* BESSIE *goes on clearing the table, taking toast-rack, butter and marmalade to the trolley.* BEECHAM *comes back as the car is heard to drive away.*)

BEECHAM. ' Safe trip '—indeed.

BESSIE (*crossing to the table for the small plates and knives*). Well, don't you hope he comes back safe ? I'm sure I do.

BEECHAM. That's not the point. It's not your place to say so—see ?

BESSIE. No—I don't see. He's nice, his lordship is.

BEECHAM. And what's he got that I've not got ?

BESSIE. I wouldn't know him well enough to say. Not yet.

BEECHAM. What do you mean—' Not yet ' ?

BESSIE. Just what I says. Not yet.

BEECHAM. Now, don't you get ideas, my girl. You've work to do. And working people can't afford to get ideas.

BESSIE. Why can't they ? They don't get much else.

BEECHAM. You looking for a husband, eh ?

BESSIE. And if I am ?

BEECHAM. And if you are—stop looking for him right above your head. You don't find husbands in the clouds. You may find other things—not husbands, though. A woman finds her husband on the ground—and keeps him there.

BESSIE. I ain't found mine. (*She crosses to the trolley with small plates, knives and napkins.*)

BEECHAM. Maybe you haven't looked. (*He moves towards her.*) Maybe you won't find one until you've learnt to keep your place.

BESSIE (*looking at him provocatively*). Perhaps I haven't found it yet.

BEECHAM. You found your place the day that you were born. So keep it, see ? The world's arranged that way—for all of us. You don't see elephants in trees.

(*He has been getting a little nearer to* BESSIE. *Suddenly the telephone rings. He crosses* R. *to answer it.*)

Hullo ? . . . Yes . . . Mr. Cleghorn ? . . . You will be delighted to accept for next week-end. I thank you, sir. I'll tell her ladyship.

(*He hangs up and turns to* BESSIE, *who is about to leave the room with the tray.*)

That means I'll have to watch the spoons.

(BESSIE *goes out down* L. BEECHAM *goes to finish off clearing the breakfast table with a look on his face of mingled resignation, forbearance and disgust.* LORD LISTER *enters through the window, immersed in his book and still carrying the duck food. He comes to his place at the table and sits.* BEECHAM *is standing above the table, holding the coffee-pot and milk jug.*)

LORD LISTER.   Breakfast nearly ready, Beecham ?
BEECHAM.   You've had it once, my lord.
LORD LISTER.   Are you sure ?
BEECHAM.   Quite sure, my lord.
LORD LISTER.   Dammit, there's someone who hasn't—— (*He sees the duck food.*)   Oh, yes, of course, these blasted ducks. (*He gets up again to go through the window.*)

CURTAIN

ACT II

SCENE 1

The following week-end. Saturday night—after dinner.
The armchair is moved slightly towards C. *in this Scene, and the*
small table placed near the up R. *corner of it. The chair up* R. *is*
brought to R. *of the table.*
LORD LISTER *is behind the sofa, wearing a day suit.* LADY LISTER
R., *and* LADY CAROLINE L., *are seated on the sofa.* LADY LISTER
is doing some mending, and wears a short dress. LADY CAROLINE *is*
in evening dress. JUNE, *in trousers and a sweater, is sitting in the*
chair at the desk. TONY, *with open shirt and corduroy trousers, is*
sitting on the floor beside her. They are reading letters. CLEGHORN,
in a dinner jacket, is in the armchair.

LORD LISTER. Dashed sorry, Cleghorn—making you bottle yourself up in that dashed outfit. Beecham should have told you that
we didn't dress. (*He comes to* L. *of* CLEGHORN. *He has a pack of*
cards which he has picked up from the sofa table.)
CLEGHORN. That's quite all right. I always wear it, Lister.
LADY CAROLINE. It's so much nicer changing in the evenings—
after all the heat and dust of the day—the tumult and the shouting.
LORD LISTER (*moving above the armchair to* R.). Who's been
shouting, Caroline ?
LADY CAROLINE. Joe, I was quoting then.
LORD LISTER (*sitting in the chair* R. *of the small table*). Tell you
what I'll do, Cleghorn. I'll put mine on to-morrow—just for old
times' sake. My dear fellow, have a cigarette ? Tony, get your
guest a cigarette. (*He starts to play patience.*)
CLEGHORN. No, please. I never do. (*He takes out a cigar.*
To LADY LISTER.) I hope you don't mind these ?
LADY LISTER. No—not at all. No—do go on. My husband
loves the smell.
LADY CAROLINE. Well, Mr. Cleghorn—have you bought yourself
a nice job in the Cabinet ?
CLEGHORN (*refusing to take offence*). Oh, well—I live in hopes.
The Chief approached me on the question when the Coalition first
broke up.
LADY LISTER. Oh, how exciting—tell me, which post do you
fancy ?
CLEGHORN. Don't ask me !
LADY LISTER. Why not Prime Minister ?
CLEGHORN. Afraid that's booked.
LADY CAROLINE. And, anyway, one needs a wife for that.
CLEGHORN. You think that's an essential ?
LADY CAROLINE. Yes, of course. Responsibility doesn't go with

29

bachelordom. What you need is an old Conservative wife to knock you into shape and file the edges down.

CLEGHORN. You find me rough ?

LADY CAROLINE. No—just uncut.

LORD LISTER. Tell me, Cleghorn—are you in favour of this State Control ?

CLEGHORN. In certain cases, yes.

LORD LISTER. What, all the usual stuff ? The mines—the banks—so forth ?

CLEGHORN. Yes, broadly speaking, yes.

LORD LISTER. I looked your manifesto through. Not one dashed word about the land.

CLEGHORN. Oh, well. I'm glad I pleased you by default.

LORD LISTER. You didn't please me, man. If someone doesn't take this blasted place away before I die, my wife'll have to walk the streets.

LADY LISTER. Joe, don't be silly, dear. I've got my ducks.

LORD LISTER. You won't have, dear, if I don't shoot that fox. (*To* CLEGHORN.) You wouldn't want the land controlled, is that correct ?

CLEGHORN. No, rather not. Not yet. We can't sweep everything inside the State at once.

LORD LISTER. But, dash it, man. It's common decency. You tax me nineteen shillings in the pound—and more—and then expect me to keep up a place like Blenheim, Fontainebleu and Versailles all rolled into one.

LADY CAROLINE. Why don't you let it, Joe ?

LORD LISTER. Beecham wouldn't stand for it. And, anyway, who'd take it ? Takes you half an hour to run your bath. The food's cold when it reaches you. Why, dash it all, you need a horse to get around these corridors.

JUNE. Say, this is good. Say, listen. ' Dear Lord Pym,—May I say how sorry, etc., etc., etc. May I also echo—in the words of your grand old father, quoted in the current *Advertiser*—we must fight back.'

TONY. Here, who sent that ?

LADY LISTER. You didn't say that, Joe ?

LORD LISTER. Say what, my dear ?

JUNE. Say, Joe, have you been spouting to the Press ?

LADY LISTER. Of course he hasn't, June ; he's only written to the papers once. *The Times.* About young women's toenails.

(TONY *rises and moves up* R.)

LORD LISTER. Painting 'em—you know.

CLEGHORN. That's interesting. What line did you take ?

LORD LISTER. I merely pointed out that people did it—just before the fall of Rome. Dashed fellow never put it in. He sent it back. He said he thought there were other more strategic reasons why

Rome fell. Facetious ass. Of course, they may be better now
they're red.

JUNE.   What colour were they then ?

LADY LISTER.   No, dear.   He means *The Times.*

(BEECHAM *comes in down* L. *for the coffee-cups.*)

TONY.   Oh, Beecham, could you get the *Advertiser* for this week ?

BEECHAM.   Yes, very good, my lord.

LORD LISTER.   I put it by the raspberries to keep the birds away.

BEECHAM.   Oh, yes, my lord.

(BEECHAM *goes out down* L.)

LORD LISTER (*to* CLEGHORN).   By the way, talking of the
Advertiser, I saw a bit last week where you described me as a parasite.
Mark you, I'm not complaining.   Something in it, I daresay.

LADY LISTER.   What nonsense, Joe.   It only said the family
should not monopolize this Seat.

TONY (*crossing* C.).   By Jove, it's right at that.   I couldn't say so,
Cleghorn, at the time.   But still, I couldn't help agreeing with you
all along the line.

JUNE.   Stop shooting off your mouth.

TONY.   After all, just because one of our ancestors picked up a
damned good pocket borough—paid through the nose for it—got a
majority of two in an electorate of ten, by bribery—it doesn't mean
that I'm prepared to carry on where he left off.

LADY LISTER.   But then you didn't, did you, dear ?

CLEGHORN.   Now, Pym, you shouldn't talk like that.   A man in
your position's got so much to give.

TONY (*sitting on the* R. *arm of the sofa*).   Afraid that's where you're
wrong.   I gave eight hundred quid—and that's the lot.

LORD LISTER.   And that was mine.

CLEGHORN.   Of course, my party pays its candidates' expenses.

TONY.   Really ?

CLEGHORN.   Yes.

TONY.   I say !

(BEECHAM *enters through the french windows with the* Advertiser,
and comes down R.)

JUNE.   Oh, let me see it, Beecham.   Be a pal.

BEECHAM.   Would that be the item, miss ?   (*He gives it to her.*)

LORD LISTER.   I want my evening clothes to-morrow, Beecham.

BEECHAM.   If your lordship recollects, you gave them to the
gamekeeper last year.

LORD LISTER.   Well, dash it, he won't want 'em every night.

BEECHAM.   No, no, my lord.   Your lordship gave them to him
with a view to scaring off the pigeons from the plums.

JUNE (*who has been reading*).   I say, that's swell.   That's really
swell.

(BEECHAM *takes the coffee-cups at the desk to the table above the sofa.*)

LADY LISTER. What is it, June ? Don't keep it to yourself.
JUNE. All tuned in ?

(BEECHAM, *in the background, listens proudly.*)

(*Reading.*) ' Lord Lister, in a recent statement from Lister Castle, made the following comment on the defeat of his son, Lord Pym, in the General Election. " ——As Lord Lieutenant, I am neutral. As a man, I feel the situation most acutely. The effect on the human organism of two hundred years' tradition overthrown as suddenly as this is hard to gorge at first—— " '

BEECHAM. ' Gauge,' miss. (*He collects the coffee-cup from the small table* R.C.)

JUNE. ' " Gauge " at first—— All I can say is that the mind is numbed, while kindly Nature breathes her healing balm around her stricken child.'

LADY LISTER. Joe, you only had one glass of sherry and a Guinness on that day.

JUNE. This is IT. ' His lordship closed with the stirring call to battle. " We must fight back," he said, " WE MUST FIGHT BACK." ' (*Running to* LORD LISTER *and throwing her arms round his neck.*) You sweetie-pie ! I wish I was engaged to you instead of Tony.

LORD LISTER. Yes, my dear—so do I. (*He disengages himself.*) Beecham, have I ever written for the *Advertiser* ?

BEECHAM. To my knowledge, no, my lord.

LORD LISTER. Well—who the devil has ?

BEECHAM. If I may hazard a suggestion, my lord, I would say that the paragraph in question has been contributed by some un-known Elector, with a view to bolstering morale beneath the heavy shadow of defeat. (*He moves down to the door.*)

TONY. Yes, that's the thing. To get a bit of easy cash.

BEECHAM (*turning*). There are Conservatives, my lord, whose motives on occasion are not prompted by the lust for gold.

(BEECHAM *goes out down* L. *with the coffee tray and cups.* JUNE *glances at the* Advertiser *again, then after a short while puts it on the table up* R.C.)

LADY CAROLINE. How nice he is. He gives one confidence.

LORD LISTER (*to* CLEGHORN). My sister's a Conservative, you see. Museum minded. Still believes in aristocracies.

LADY CAROLINE. I'm sure Mr. Cleghorn does as well.

CLEGHORN. Oh, no. You saw my speech in Lister Market, didn't you ?

LADY LISTER. Of course, that's why I voted for you.

CLEGHORN. What ! Against your own son ?

LADY LISTER. Oh, yes. We take no part in Party Politics.

CLEGHORN. You sabotage them, eh ?

LADY CAROLINE. Why don't you like the aristocracy, may I ask ?
CLEGHORN. Oh, many reasons.
JUNE (*in the background,* C.). Because you aren't a belted Earl yourself ?
LADY LISTER. Now, June dear, don't be rude.
CLEGHORN. I merely think the aristocracy's out of date.
JUNE. Oh, hell, you make me sick. (*Looking towards the fire-place.*) That picture's old. You don't chuck that away because it's old.
CLEGHORN. That's just an ornament, Miss June.
JUNE. So what ! What's wrong with ornaments? I'm one myself.
CLEGHORN. A very pretty one, if I may say so.
JUNE. You think I'm out of date ?
CLEGHORN. No, God forbid.
TONY. I do. I never heard such concentrated rot in all my life.
JUNE (*turning on him*). You got engaged 'cos I'm an ornament—or was it for my cash ?
LADY LISTER. Now, June, don't get so overwrought. You can't turn everything to personalities.
JUNE (*turning away above the armchair to* R.). You can. That's what they are. That's life. The rest's just fossils and machines.
LORD LISTER. Tory fossils and Socialist machines ?
LADY CAROLINE. I really think it's time we went to bed.

(*The telephone rings.*)

JUNE (*answering it*). Hullo, who's calling ? . . . Yeah, Lister Castle . . . O.K. Who's on the line ? . . .
LADY LISTER. I think it's time we all went up. (*To* CLEGHORN.) I expect you'll have a lot of all-night sittings in the House.
CLEGHORN. Yes, we've got a lot to do to straighten out the world.
LADY LISTER. Be very careful with it—won't you ? It's a little brittle, I'm afraid.
JUNE. Oh, say, HULLO ! How are you ? What's the story ? . . . Yes, I am. American . . . Say, how'd you guess ? . . . I'm going to marry a Conservative. Lord Pym. You ever heard of him ? . . . You have ? . . . You think he's good ? I think he's dumb. Well, guess you're busy, so I'll pass you on—— Oh, hey ! I'm very sorry that you won. (*She turns to* CLEGHORN.) A guy called Attlee calling you.
LADY LISTER. Attlee !

(CLEGHORN *rises and takes the receiver.* TONY *rises and comes to above the table* R.C. *and watches* LORD LISTER'S *game.*)

CLEGHORN. Hullo ? . . . Yes, Chief. It's Cleghorn here . . . What's that ? . . . I'm very honoured. I'll be delighted . . .

Rather. That suits me . . . What's that ? . . . No, Clem, no—I can't accept . . . I'm sorry, no. Against my principles.

LADY LISTER. Now, Mr. Cleghorn, principles need not be obstacles, you know.

CLEGHORN (*taking a snap decision*). Well, Clem, if you put it like that I can't refuse . . . Well, thanks . . . That's fine. See you next week . . . Good-night. (*He hangs up.*)

LADY LISTER. What is it, Mr. Cleghorn ?

CLEGHORN. He's offered me the Dominions.

LADY LISTER. Accepted ?

CLEGHORN. Yes.

LADY LISTER. You must be pleased. Why did you hesitate ?

CLEGHORN. Afraid he made a proviso. Too many Ministers in the Commons. So he's sent me to the Lords.

JUNE. You turned that down ?

CLEGHORN. I took it, no.

JUNE. You can't have done. You said just now——

CLEGHORN (*rather embarrassed*). Well, it was just the way he put it.

JUNE. P'raps the P.M. in Queen Anne's day put it just like that.

LADY LISTER. Not on the telephone, I'm sure he didn't, dear.

LORD LISTER (*rising*). What'll you call yourself, Cleghorn ? (*He goes to the table behind the sofa and pours two drinks.*)

CLEGHORN. Oh, Cleghorn's good enough for me. (*He sits in the armchair again.*)

LADY CAROLINE. It has to be OF somewhere, doesn't it ?

LADY LISTER. I think it does. Where do you live ?

CLEGHORN. At Egham, I'm afraid.

LORD LISTER. It can't be helped.

LADY LISTER. That means a by-election, doesn't it ?

JUNE. What, HERE ?

LADY LISTER. Yes, dear, the sitting Member's gone up to the House of Lords.

JUNE. But Tony here's a Lord.

LORD LISTER. That's courtesy, my dear, that's all. It doesn't count. Eldest son, that's all. He's really Anthony Smith—only some dashed fellow at the College of Heralds wants something to do.

(*He hands* CLEGHORN *a drink, then returns to the sofa table for his own.*)

JUNE. A by-election here ! Say, Tony, that's your chance. A second chance. Oh, gee !

TONY. I've told you, June—I've had the Tories.

LADY LISTER. Well then, you ought to stand as Labour candidate instead of Mr. Cleghorn—don't you think so ?

CLEGHORN. That depends on Pym.

TONY (*interested*). You think that one could change like that ?

CLEGHORN. Well, people do.

LORD LISTER. Of course they do. Winston did. I always think chameleons make dashed good M.P.'s.

BEECHAM *enters down* L. *with a glass of water on a salver and goes to* L. *of* LADY CAROLINE.)

BEECHAM. Your glass of hot water, Lady Caroline.
LADY CAROLINE. A little whisky, please—to celebrate.

(BEECHAM *moves up to get the whisky.*)

JUNE. Say, Tony, if you change I'll never speak to you again.
TONY. You told me that I had to find a job.
JUNE. I'm just not kidding, Tony. (*She kisses him.*) I'll NEVER speak to you again.
LORD LISTER. My dear Caroline, I've never seen you touch the stuff before.

(BEECHAM *brings the whisky to* LADY CAROLINE.)

LADY CAROLINE. My dear Joseph, I've never heard a charming man like Mr. Cleghorn so honoured before. (*She sips the whisky.*) It's very strong. I think I'll finish it upstairs. (*Rising.*) I'm ready now, Molly. Goodnight.
LADY LISTER (*rising*). I'm coming with you. Goodnight, everybody. Goodnight, Mr. Cleghorn. I do hope you'll be comfortable.
CLEGHORN (*who has risen*). I hope so.
LADY LISTER. Goodnight, Joe. Don't sit up too late.

BEECHAM *holds open the door, and* LADY LISTER *and* LADY CAROLINE *go out down* L. CLEGHORN *crosses to the sofa and sits.* BEECHAM *is about to go out when* JUNE *breaks in.*)

JUNE. Say, Beecham, there's a by-election here.
BEECHAM. Has Mr. Cleghorn had an accident, then, miss ?
TONY. He has. He's going to the House of Lords.
JUNE. Well, Beecham, how's it hit you ? Pretty good ?
BEECHAM. I understand that Mr. Asquith contemplated something similar in 1911, miss—on a somewhat larger scale.
CLEGHORN. Oh, Beecham, I've rather a busy day to-morrow. Could I have an early call ?
BEECHAM. I'll mention it to Bessie, sir.
CLEGHORN. Six-thirty ?
BEECHAM. Very good, MY LORD.

(*He goes out down* L. *with an icy look on his face.*)

TONY (*crossing to the sofa*). Have another drink ?
CLEGHORN. No, thanks. (*He puts his glass on the table behind him.*)

TONY. Now, what about this by-election, sir ? (*He sits* R. *of* CLEGHORN *on the sofa.*)

CLEGHORN. Well, what about it, Pym ?

TONY. If I did stand as Labour . . .

JUNE (*cannot take this*). Say, Joe, come out around the garden and I'll drive the foxes over you.

LORD LISTER. Eh, what ? (*He sees the situation.*) All right— I doubt if I'll hit the beggar on the move and in the dark. (*He picks up his rifle.*) Still, try anything once.

JUNE. It's guys who haven't got the pep to try things twice that get my goat.

(LORD LISTER *and* JUNE *go out through the french window.*)

CLEGHORN. You're just a bit unpopular, I think.

TONY. Oh, typical American. Old fashioned—' Ghost Goes West '—and all that stuff. Now, what about this Seat ? You got a candidate ?

CLEGHORN (*laughing*). The Labour Party moves quite fast—but not as fast as that.

TONY. Got one in mind ?

CLEGHORN. I mustn't give information away to the enemy.

TONY. Don't worry about me. I've had the Right.

CLEGHORN. Then you were serious to-night ?

TONY. Of course. So's Father—Mother too. One must progress.

CLEGHORN. Pym, are you genuinely Left ? Or are you Left— well, just because the Right's got left behind ?

TONY. Oh, no. It's genuine.

CLEGHORN. Quite sure ?

TONY. I know I stood as a Conservative, but—dash it all—one must progress. This election's taught me something. Every dashed question had me. ' Why should you be a lord ? ' Well, why should I ? Damn it, they'll ask YOU that to-morrow.

CLEGHORN. Let's stick to the point. Your election address made me think. You didn't what you might call ' quote the Tory Press.' If you'd been a Liberal, I would have said, well—vote-catching. But as you were a Tory, I thought, well—this boy's sincere.

TONY. You did ? Well, thank God someone did.

CLEGHORN. Sincere—but not a Tory, do you see. (*Rising and crossing to the desk.*) Now, Pym, I'll tell you what I'll do. I'm speaking as a politician now. I'll call the Party Secretary. (*He sits on the desk and takes up the receiver.*) Of course, it's not my pigeon now, but still, I take it I'll still pull some weight. (*Into the telephone.*) Lister 2911, please. (*To* TONY.) You're sure you mean it, Pym ?

TONY. Yes, rather, yes.

CLEGHORN. Your fiancée ?

TONY. Oh, she'll be all right.

CLEGHORN. She's obstinate.

TONY. Well, damn it, so am I. I'm dashed if I'll live on her.

CLEGHORN. All right. But still, she doesn't look the type who's keen on unconditional surrender—— (*Into the telephone.*) Oh, hello. Cleghorn here . . . Look, I've some news for you. I'm going to the Upper House . . . Dominions . . . Oh, thanks . . . Yes, rather a surprise in a way . . . That's very decent of you—thanks. Now look . . . Exactly . . . Yes, that's what I've called you up about . . .

(JUNE *has come in and is standing by the window.*)

Yes, I have. I've thought about it quite a bit . . . Yes, well—well, I suggest young Pym . . . Yes, yes, I think he would. And it would save a contest . . . Quite . . . Yes, National—or something of that sort. The Tories often try that trick . . . Well, anyway, you sleep on it. I'll see you Monday morning . . . Yes, and many thanks again . . . Goodnight. (*He hangs up and rises.*)

(LORD LISTER *enters through the french window.*)

LORD LISTER. Well, I'm off to bed. Coming, Cleghorn? Never saw the brute. (*Putting his rifle by the window.*) I smelt him, though. I don't suppose it comes out, anyway, until I've gone to bed. (*Crossing down* L.) You coming up?

CLEGHORN (*crossing* L.). Yes, rather, yes. Goodnight, Pym.

TONY (*rising*). Goodnight—and thank you.

CLEGHORN. Thumbs up. Goodnight, Miss Farrell.

(JUNE *does not answer.* CLEGHORN *goes out down* L.)

LORD LISTER. Don't sit up all night, Tony. And shut that window. Don't want rabbits chewing up the chairs.

TONY. Yes. Goodnight.

(LORD LISTER *goes out down* L.)

(*Going to the table behind the sofa.*) Have a drink?

JUNE (*above the armchair*). You lousy little worm. I wouldn't marry you if I were paid a million dollars down—and free of tax.

TONY. Why? What's the matter now?

JUNE. Say, can't you guess? You surely aren't that dumb!

TONY. Me going Labour, I suppose? So that's it, is it? Silly child. You know damn all about our politics. The world moves on—that's all. One either moves as well—or gets moved out. It's providence, this break. And if they have me I'll be unopposed. Besides, this talk of party politics is all hot air. They all want just the same—they all want bread and beer and dollars. (*He walks across the room.*) The parties are just labels. Labels get worn out and can—and should—be changed. (*He crosses again to above the sofa.*)

JUNE. If there's no difference, why——

TONY. Don't be a silly kid. I'm doing this for you.

JUNE. For me! That's swell! Say, thanks a lot!

TONY. You told me I must get a job. You told me I must rough it, like your uncles in the States. And so I've joined the Labour Party. Damn it—if that isn't roughing it, what is ? (*He moves towards her.*) Come here, don't be a silly little ass. Come on—let's have a kiss. All right, I'll come to you.

(*She turns away down* R.)

All right, if you're going to be a child—well, carry on. If one does something in one's life that one believes in, people always turn against one anyway. One's got to bear one's cross.

JUNE. O.K. St. Anthony !

TONY (*moving towards her again*). June—please—I want to kiss you, please.

JUNE. I wouldn't want to kiss a yellow skunk.

TONY (*turning up to the window*). All right, I'll shoot myself. (*He picks up the rifle.*) You'd look pretty silly if I shot myself because you couldn't mind your business. What would you do ?

JUNE. I guess I'd tell your father that another rabbit's had it in the grounds.

(TONY *goes out through the french window.* JUNE *flops down in the armchair.* BEECHAM *enters down* L.)

JUNE. Oh, Beecham, come and hold my hand. I want my mum.

BEECHAM. I doubt if I should be a satisfactory substitute for Mrs. Farrell, miss.

JUNE. Give me a drink. Have one yourself. (*As he hesitates.*) Go on. Relax. The upper class have gone to bed.

(BEECHAM *pours out two drinks at the table above the sofa.*)

You ought to meet my mother, Beecham. You'd be nuts about her. Doesn't stink of autumn leaves, like all the guys round here.

BEECHAM (*crossing to her with the two drinks*). She sounds refreshing, miss. (*He hands her one glass, then lifts the other.*) To your engagement, miss—the union of two great English-speaking Powers.

JUNE. One isn't speaking, Beecham. My engagement's off.

BEECHAM. A lovers' tiff, miss, frequently occurs in the pre-nuptial period.

JUNE. Say, Beecham, would you marry Tony ?

BEECHAM. Well, miss, if I were young and beautiful and rich——

JUNE. If you wore skirts and he wore pants, would you get hitched ?

BEECHAM. I would, miss—on the long view—yes. His lordship is perhaps a trifle immature. The public school system in vogue in this country has a tendency towards prolonging adolescence into early manhood, miss.

JUNE. I'll say it has.

BEECHAM. May I enquire if you feel amatory towards his lordship, miss ?

JUNE. Hell, Beecham—cut the parlour talk. You asking—' Am I nuts about the guy ? '

BEECHAM. That phrase contains in essence the embodiment of my enquiry, miss.

JUNE (*rising and going down* R.). Oh, I dunno. (*She considers.*) I want to bite his ears till the room spins round and all his ancestors stand up inside their frames and shout out ' Atta girl '—You follow me ?

BEECHAM. Quite closely, miss.

JUNE. I want to go away and never see the dope again. I want to hug him—till his ribs are cracked. I want to slap his face and pull his hair and kick him in the teeth. I want—— (*Crossing to* BEECHAM.) Oh, Beecham, tell me what I want.

BEECHAM. I think, miss, if you'll pardon me, you want a good night's rest.

JUNE. But do I love the guy ?

BEECHAM. His lordship certainly appears to play a major rôle in your emotional reactions, miss.

JUNE. But if he stands as Labour in the by-election—that's the end.

BEECHAM. I think it most unlikely, miss. His lordship lacks political stability, admittedly—but surely not to that extent.

JUNE. That's what you think. It's all arranged. (*She sits on the sofa.*)

BEECHAM (*amazed*). You mean that, miss ?

JUNE. Yeah. Have another drink.

(BEECHAM *goes to the table above the sofa and pours himself another whisky.*)

It knocks Pearl Harbour through the hoop.

BEECHAM. Exactly, miss—that episode assumes the relative importance of a fracas in a public-house.

JUNE. Oh, Beecham. What am I to do ?

BEECHAM. I suggest you fight him back, miss.

(*She looks up.*)

Remember Lady Astor was a foreigner, and yet she sometimes gained the public ear.

JUNE. But Lady Astor married. I'm a U.S. citizen.

BEECHAM. That's easily adjusted, miss.

JUNE. Say, Beecham, are you doing the big thing ?

BEECHAM. No, miss. His lordship was the groom I had in mind.

JUNE. What—board him first—and sink him afterwards ?

BEECHAM. Precisely, miss.

JUNE. We aren't on speaking terms.

BEECHAM. I should be very ready, miss, to take the rôle of go-between.

JUNE. No. Hell, I won't. He's letting down the family—betraying everything he ought to love, including me.

BEECHAM. In that event, miss, nothing can be done. Except to wait and trust to the Electorate to show his lordship that expediency does not always pay. (*He puts down his glass on the table above the sofa.*)

JUNE. But Mr. Cleghorn says he'll be unopposed.

BEECHAM. It's up to someone to oppose him, miss.

JUNE. But WHO ?

BEECHAM. I don't know, miss. The situation's terrible. There's nothing I would not do to save his lordship from political advancement at the cost of principle—no, nothing, miss.

JUNE. Say, is that true ?

BEECHAM (*surprised at the tone in her voice*). Indeed it is, miss, yes.

JUNE. O.K. Oh, Beecham, you're swell—Beecham. Does your mother call you Beecham too ?

BEECHAM. No, miss. She calls me Benjamin. Beecham was my mother's maiden name. My father's name—my proper name—is Charles. Benjamin Charles.

JUNE. That's swell. Why Benjamin ?

BEECHAM. My father's father had a great affection for the late Lord Beaconsfield——

JUNE. Your grandmother ?

BEECHAM. I said—grandfather—miss.

JUNE (*rising*). Oh, yeah. Of course you did. (*She moves up round the end of the sofa to* L. *of him.*) Now, Benjy—we've a secret—you and I—till Nomination Day.

BEECHAM. What secret, miss ?

JUNE. His lordship's going to be opposed ! That's all. Good-night. (*She kisses his cheek, crosses down* L., *then turns at the door.*) And keep your chin up. We'll fight them back !

(JUNE *goes out.* BEECHAM *picks up his glass and swallows the remainder of his drink.* TONY *enters through the french window with the rifle, which he leaves up* R.C.)

TONY. Hey, Beecham, leave that there. I want a drink. (*He comes* C.)

BEECHAM. I thought perhaps you would, my lord. I'll pour it out. (*He pours whisky into a glass.*)

TONY. No soda, thanks. (*He takes it from* BEECHAM.) I may be going to fight this seat as Labour—have you heard ? Dashed good idea, what ?

BEECHAM. That's open to debate, my lord.

TONY. Well, dash it—everybody's Labour now. Call myself

National Labour—and get twenty thousand Labour votes—and most of the Conservative. Besides, I'll be unopposed.

BEECHAM. Perhaps, my lord.

TONY. Don't tell me anybody'd be such a silly fool as to fight me and lose his deposit.

BEECHAM. It's the so-called silly fools that often save the world, my lord. (*He crosses down* L.)

TONY. What for—that's what I want to know—what for?

BEECHAM (*turning at the door*). Posterity, my lord. Good night.

{*He goes out down* L. TONY *goes to the window up* R.C. *After a pause,* BESSIE *enters down* L. *She sees* TONY.)

BESSIE. My lord. I seen the light.

TONY. You have, by Jove? I've seen it too.

BESSIE. I came to put it out.

TONY. Oh, yes. Well, carry on. (*He puts his glass on the table* R.C. *and switches off the lamp.*) It's nicer in the dark. (*He moves down towards her.*)

BESSIE (*backing from him*). I thought that there was no one here.

TONY. Now, don't keep walking backwards, Bessie. You'll have a fall. Sit down and have a chat.

BESSIE. Oh, sir, I couldn't, sir.

TONY. Why couldn't you? Come on. (*As* BESSIE *moves towards the sofa.*) Sit down and have a drink.

(BESSIE *sits at* L. *end of the sofa.* TONY *goes to the drink table to pour out a drink for her.*)

I want to hear your views on politics. You voted for old Cleghorn, didn't you?

BESSIE. I'm sorry, yes, my lord.

TONY (*coming round* R. *of the sofa*). Good show! You've got some sense. (*He hands her the drink.*) That not too strong?

(*She nods.*)

(*Sitting beside her,* R., *and offering his case.*) A cigarette?

BESSIE. No thanks, my lord.

TONY. Don't smoke?

BESSIE. No, sir.

TONY. You funny child, what do you do?

BESSIE. I do the rooms, my lord.

TONY. Oh, yes, I know you do. Dashed well, as well. There's going to be a by-election here.

BESSIE. Oh, yes, my lord.

TONY. I'm going to stand as Labour, possibly.

BESSIE. Oh, I'm glad.

TONY. You are? Thank heaven someone is. Now, tell me why.

BESSIE. Then I can vote for you, my lord. Just like I wanted to.

TONY. Why did you want to, eh?

BESSIE. Oh, sir !

TONY. Because you liked my face ?

BESSIE (*turning away*). Oh, sir !

TONY. That's awfully sweet. (*He rises and takes her empty glass to the drink table.*) Another one ?

BESSIE. Oh, sir—I mustn't, sir.

TONY. Come on. Why not ? (*Pouring her another one even stronger than the last.*) Now, Bessie, what's your plan in life ?

BESSIE. Oh, sir, I haven't thought——

TONY. Of course you have. All women think—of that. How old are you ? (*He comes down to her.*)

BESSIE. I'm twenty-two.

TONY. A boy friend, eh ? (*He hands her glass.*)

BESSIE. No, sir.

TONY. A man friend, then. (*He sits beside her again.*) I know all about you. You don't believe in marriage, do you ?

BESSIE. Oh, I do.

TONY. You mustn't, Bessie, it's all rot. One can't get unconditional surrender from a woman.

BESSIE. Sir, you mustn't talk like that.

TONY. Why not ? It's true.

BESSIE. Miss June——

TONY. Blow Miss June. She's given me the bird.

BESSIE. I'm sorry, sir.

TONY. How sweet you are. What pretty hands you've got. You mustn't spoil them dusting. (*He tries to take one, unsuccessfully.*) Damn it all, why should you dust ? Mother does it, anyway.

BESSIE. I've got to earn my keep.

TONY. I know, it all comes down to that. You don't believe in money, do you, being Commonwealth ?

BESSIE. Well, it's nice to have a bit.

TONY. It isn't, Bessie. It can't buy the only thing that matters —which is love. You wouldn't like to hold my hand ?

BESSIE. Oh, sir.

TONY. Of course you wouldn't—no. I'm feeling lonely, that was all. You ought to fall in love and settle down. A little cottage —and some flowers.

BESSIE. Yes, sir—it would be nice.

TONY. Don't call me ' sir.' Tony's my name.

BESSIE. Oh, sir—I couldn't, sir.

TONY. Of course you could. You said you couldn't have a drink. You've had two now. (*He takes her glass and puts it on the table behind.*) Come on—say Tony twice.

BESSIE. Tony.

TONY. Again.

BESSIE. Tony. (*She giggles.*) Oh, it's so funny here.

TONY. What's funny ? Me ?

BESSIE. The place. It's all so big. I live at home in just a tiny cottage. Father, Mother, me—that's all. It's nicer, though. It's much more homely. People are themselves. It's cheaper, too.

TONY. How much?

BESSIE. Well, ours is nine and six a week.

TONY. Good God—can people live in a cottage for nine and six a week?

BESSIE. Of course, you can have smaller ones.

TONY. How sweet and sensible you are. A cottage and some flowers is all one wants. Except, of course, a wife.

BESSIE. That might be more expensive.

TONY. Why? It needn't be. (*He puts an arm round her.*) It wouldn't be—with you.

BESSIE (*getting up*). Oh, sir—I'm going to bed.

TONY (*getting up too*). What's wrong? Don't go. I think you're sweet. (*He suddenly kisses her.*)

BESSIE (*bursting into tears*). Oh, sir.

TONY. What's up?

BESSIE. I didn't ever want to till I met my man.

TONY. Well, p'raps you have. And, anyway, you've got to start sometime.

BESSIE. It's not your fault. I'll just go up.

TONY. No, Bessie, stop. I didn't want to spoil your dream.

BESSIE. I know. But—just the same—it's spoiled.

TONY. Well—if it's spoiled—let's have another one to say ' Goodnight. ' (*He holds out his arms to her and she comes into them.*) Perhaps we haven't spoilt your dream after all.

(*They both sink on to the sofa and continue with the embrace.* LORD LISTER *enters down* L. *in a dressing gown, and crosses below the sofa to the window.*)

LORD LISTER. Hullo, Tony. You still up? (*He picks up his rifle.*) Came to get my gun.

(TONY *and* BESSIE *rise.*)

Moonlight. I might see something from my dressing-room. (*He discerns another figure.*) Hullo, is that June?

TONY. No, Father. Do you know Miss Sykes? (*Lamely.*) She's Commonwealth.

LORD LISTER (*crossing and shaking hands with* BESSIE). Oh, howd' you do? Dashed good of you to turn out at this time of night. You politicians never rest. I mustn't hang about, or Molly's sure to see a bat. Molly's my wife. She can't stand bats. She thinks they nest in women's hair. God knows why! I wouldn't like to have my nest brushed twice a day. And hair-pins shoved right through me. Still, one never knows with bats. Well, I'll be off. Call again and meet my wife. (*He goes to the door, then turns.*) Say, tea—or something. Sorry she's not down to see you now.

(*He examines his equipment.*)   I got everything ?   Mustn't interrupt
you.   I expect you want to go on chewing over the Election.   Well,
goodnight.

(*He exits down* L.)

CURTAIN

ACT II

SCENE 2

Nomination Day in the By-election.
    The Scene is set for breakfast as in Act I, *Scene* 2.   BESSIE, *the
silver basket on her arm, is putting the finishing touches to the table.*
TONY *enters down* L. *in a smart city suit.*

TONY.   'Morning, Bessie.   (*As she just stands and looks at him.*)
What's the matter—have you lost your voice ?
    BESSIE.   I'm sure I don't know what I've lost, my lord.
    TONY (*going up to kiss her*).   Come on, let's see you smile.   I'll
be an M.P. by one o'clock.
    BESSIE.   I thought they had to vote.
    TONY.   Not when I'm unopposed.   Come on, let's have a kiss.

(*They kiss.*)

You liked that, didn't you ?
    BESSIE.   I like a lot of things I didn't like before.
    TONY.   Then you must be in love.
    BESSIE.   Well, p'raps I am.
    TONY.   With me ?

(BESSIE *pulls away.*)

What's the matter ?
    BESSIE (*bursting into tears*).   Oh, I don't know.   I wish I knew.
(*She turns away to* R. *of the sofa.*)
    TONY.   No, Bessie.   Not at breakfast, please.

(*She rushes to the door down* L., *crying.* BEECHAM *comes in with the
coffee.*)

    BEECHAM.   Here, what's the game ?
    BESSIE.   I've got a headache, sir.

(*She rushes out, leaving the door open.*)

    BEECHAM (*shouting after her*).   Well, take an aspirin and get laid
down.   (*Seeing* TONY.)   Good morning, my lord.   (*He puts the
coffee on the trolley.*)   A most emotional young person.   She informs

me that she often dreams of Mr. Errol Flynn. A trans-Atlantic cinematograph performer, I believe, my lord. (*He moves down and shuts the door.*)

TONY (*crossing to the trolley*). The papers come yet ?

BEECHAM. No, not yet, my lord. (*He returns to the trolley.*)

TONY (*strolling to the window*). It's a lovely day for politics. (BEECHAM *does not reply.*) You don't approve of Viscount Pym, M.P. ?

BEECHAM. I don't like turncoats, no, my lord. (*He brings the coffee to the table.*)

TONY. Oh, come on, Beecham ; after all, I'm unopposed. I've saved the Government a bit of cash. Besides, you voted for me as a Tory, so it shows you think I ought to be in Parliament. I've chosen the best vehicle, that's all.

BEECHAM. Talking of vehicles, the tumbril had, at least, a certain dignity, my lord.

TONY. By Jove, a revolutionary ! Is that it ? Want to guillotine us all ?

BEECHAM. Not indiscriminately, no, my lord. (*He crosses to the door down* L.)

TONY. Damn fools, those fellows. All those French aristocrats. It serves 'em right. They couldn't see the future, that was all.

BEECHAM (*above the door*). Perhaps their lack of foresight might have been less tragic than the vision of the Corsican, my lord.

TONY. What Corsican ?

BEECHAM. The Emperor Bonaparte—a somewhat irresponsible young man, my lord.

(LADY LISTER *comes in down* L.)

BEECHAM (*holding the door open*). Good morning, my lady.

LADY LISTER. Good morning, Beecham. 'Morning, Tony.

(BEECHAM *exits down* L.)

Goodness, you're early. What's the matter ? Did you drink too much last night ?

TONY. No, Mother, I'm a bit excited, I suppose.

LADY LISTER. Oh, yes, of course. It's Nomination Day. I knew it was, but Joe said I was talking nonsense. (*She has moved to the trolley.*) Oh, what squashy sausages ! (*She turns away.*) Your father's very worried, Tony dear. (*She crosses to above* R. *of the table.*)

TONY. That means you are. What's the matter ? Ducks not laying well ?

LADY LISTER. No, June. (*She kisses* TONY.) She seems so strange. She's always telephoning secretly and going out. Your father wonders—are you still engaged ? (*She sits* R. *of the table and starts her breakfast.*)

TONY. I wouldn't know. We aren't on speaking terms.

LADY LISTER. How very childish, dear ! You really must grow

up—an M.P., too, to-day.   The Speaker couldn't say I'm not on speaking terms.'

TONY.   If June would keep her fingers out of politics, I wouldn't mind.

LADY LISTER.   That's silly, dear—June's an American.   She's interested in all old-fashioned things.

TONY.   I know—I wish that isolation wasn't out of date.   (*He sits at his place at the table.*)

LADY LISTER.   Besides, she does no harm.   She's just a child.

(LORD LISTER *enters down* L. *and goes to the trolley.*)

TONY. Children can do some pretty hare-brained things.   I wouldn't trust her round the corner till I'm in—she's too dashed rich.

LORD LISTER (*helping himself to sausages*).   Who's rich ?

TONY.   June, Father.

LORD LISTER.   Why, has someone died ?

LADY LISTER.   No, dear, she's rich, that's all.   Some people are. (*She places coffee for* LORD LISTER *and* TONY.)

LORD LISTER (*coming to the table*).   Dashed funny things these death duties.   In the old days, when someone died one used to get a bit of cash.   Now someone dies and one pays up, as though it was dashed entertainment tax.   (*To* LADY LISTER, *as he sits down with his food.*)   I saw that fox last night, my dear—twelve thirty-one.

(BEECHAM *enters with the daily papers.*)

TONY.   Oh, give 'em here.   I want to see what dear Lord Beaverbrook says about me.

(BEECHAM *crosses and gives the papers to* TONY.)

LADY LISTER.   You needn't worry about that, my dear.   In 1939 he said there wouldn't be a war.

LORD LISTER.   Beecham.

BEECHAM.   Yes, my lord?

LORD LISTER.   Who cooked these sausages ?

BEECHAM.   Bessie, my lord.

LORD LISTER.   She dashed well didn't.

BEECHAM.   Very good, my lord.

LORD LISTER.   Tell Bessie from me that both sides of a sausage ought to be cooked.   (*Handing his plate to* BEECHAM.)   Take 'em back and get 'em done.

BEECHAM.   Yes, very well, my lord.   (*He makes for the door.*)

TONY (*leaping up*).   My God !

(JUNE *enters down* L.)

LADY LISTER.   What is it, dear—one of my pins ?

TONY.   I'm going to be opposed.   Listen.   (*He reads excitedly from the* Daily Express.   BEECHAM *stands listening* L.C. ;   JUNE

down L.) 'Surprise nomination expected at East Milton. Our
Political Correspondent understands that the East Milton Conservative Association have adopted as their candidate in the by-election
a well-known local figure.'

LADY LISTER.   How exciting, Tony. Is it somebody we know?

TONY. I've never heard of him. A chap called Charles.
Benjamin Charles.

(BEECHAM *drops the plate and sausages.*)

LORD LISTER.   What the devil are you doing, Beecham? Had a
heart-attack?

BEECHAM.   No, something burnt my finger-tips, my lord.

JUNE (*helping him pick up the bits*). Come on, I'll help you,
Beecham. (*Aside.*) Stick it, Benjy. 'On the beaches, in the
meadows.' Stick it, Benjy. Show you've got some guts.

LORD LISTER.   Leave him alone, June. Damn fellow comes in
here and throws the plates about. You wouldn't do that music-hall
turn in the pantry, would you, now?

BEECHAM.   Not voluntarily, no, my lord.

LORD LISTER.   Well, damn it—why try out your parlour tricks in
here? Now take 'em out and get 'em cleaned and cooked.

(BEECHAM *goes out down* L. *with the dish from the trolley and plate*,
JUNE *opening the door for him.*)

TONY (*taking the* Daily Mail). Let's see what it says here. Ah,
here's a photograph.

LADY LISTER.   Do have your coffee, Tony. It's all getting cold.

TONY.   My sainted aunt! It's Beecham! Mother, look!
It's BEECHAM, Father! BEECHAM! June! Here, ring the
bloody bell.

LADY LISTER (*taking the paper from him*). TONY! If you are
going to talk like that, you take your breakfast into the smoking-
room. I will not have you using filthy words like that before your
father. (*She glances at the photograph.*)

LORD LISTER.   What's that, dear?

LADY LISTER.   He wants to ring the bell. (*She puts down the
paper in the centre of the table.*)

LORD LISTER.   You leave the bell alone. I want my sausages.

TONY.   But, Father—BEECHAM! Standing against ME!

LORD LISTER.   Dash politics. I want my bloody sausages. (*He
picks up the paper.*)

LADY LISTER.   Yes, Tony dear, your father wants his sausages.
Sit down and have your breakfast, dear. There must be some
mistake. Perhaps Lord Beaverbrook has got things wrong again.

TONY.   And Kemsley—and Camrose—and Rothermere! Not
likely, eh?

(JUNE *crosses to above* LORD LISTER *and looks over the paper.*)

LORD LISTER (*who is studying the photo in the* Daily Mail).   Where the devil did old Beecham get that hat ?

LADY LISTER.   What's wrong with it ?   It's very smart.

LORD LISTER.   It's smart all right.   It dashed well ought to be. It cost me forty-seven shillings in St. James's Street last year.

LADY LISTER.   I gave it to him, Joe, for Christmas—I remember now.   It didn't match your suit.

LORD LISTER (*who is still studying the photograph*).   Which suit ? (*He points at the photograph with great emotion.*)   That suit ?

LADY LISTER.   Yes, dear, the suit is yours as well.   I gave that to him too.   Remember when they gave you that material—the year you won the fat-stock prize at Lister Show ?

LORD LISTER.   What !   That was priceless stuff !

LADY LISTER.   It may have been—but Beecham thought it was too loud.

(*The telephone rings.* TONY *goes to answer it.* LADY LISTER *pours coffee for* JUNE.)

TONY (*at the telephone*).   Hullo ? . . . Conservative Association ? . . . Pym here.   You don't want me ? . . . I didn't think you would. Who do you want ? . . . Miss Farrell ?   Hold the line.   Here, June. (*He holds out the receiver.*)

JUNE (*at the telephone*).   Yeah, hullo.   A lovely day for politics. . . . Yeah . . . Yeah.   I know.   We've hit the headlines quite O.K. They've done us proud.   We've jumped the gun . . . Yeah—he'll be O.K. . . . Yeah, he'll be there.   I'll keep him on the mark . . . O.K. . . .   O.K.   Be seeing you.   So long.

(*She hangs up and turns to see* TONY, *who is standing beside her with his mouth agape.*)

Hullo, you taking off the Loch Ness Monster ?

TONY.   WELL !   Dash it, June, I think you might have told me.

JUNE.   I guess I didn't kinda think you thought I was a politician, kid.

TONY.   You little fool !   My God, I wish I'd never clapped my eyes on you.

JUNE.   O.K.—Democracy !   It isn't your election, Tony. There's a crowd of other funny little guys who like to have a say. Least, that's what Lincoln thought.

TONY.   SHUT UP !

LADY LISTER.   My children, please !

TONY.   Go back and live in your stupendous, vulgar, headline-hitting country—and leave me ALONE.

(*He stamps out through the french window and walks up and down outside.*)

JUNE.   O.K.—then—Garbo.   When I've cooked your goose I'll hop it, kid. (*She goes to her place at the table, sits and starts her breakfast.*)

LADY LISTER. Now, children, please don't quarrel. There are more important things to do. (*To* LORD LISTER.) Joe, tell me—what are we to do ? You must DO something, Joe.

LORD LISTER. What can I do ? If Beecham wants to stand, it's up to him. He's twenty-one.

LADY LISTER. But, Joe, he's coming in—at any minute—with the sausages.

LORD LISTER. I hope he dashed well is.

LADY LISTER. Well, you MUST say something then.

LORD LISTER. Don't worry. If they aren't done right, I'll say a thing or two.

LADY LISTER. Oh, Joe, what use are you ?

LORD LISTER. I take no part in Party Politics, my dear.

LADY LISTER. But, dear, the servant problem isn't politics.

LORD LISTER. Still, 'course I know my duty. As Lord Lieutenant I shall have to ask him here to stay, that's—if he wins. (*Dismissing the matter from his mind.*) I saw that vixen last night, June.

JUNE. You did ? You get a shot ?

LORD LISTER. No—too dashed dark. Still, I'll get her yet. I knew a fellow once who waited for a buffalo for seven years.

JUNE. He must have been a constant guy.

LORD LISTER. Brute killed him in the end. He climbed a tree—the fella, not the buffalo. It licked his feet right off.

LADY LISTER. Joe, not at breakfast, dear !

LORD LISTER. Eh ? Not at breakfast—no. Just before dawn.

(BEECHAM *enters down* L. *with the sausages. He crosses to* LORD LISTER *with the plate and dish, puts down the plate before* LORD LISTER, *then lifts the cover of the dish for the inspection of the sausages.*)

That's better. Something like a sausage, that. (*He helps himself to a couple.*)

(BEECHAM *takes the dish back to the trolley, then goes to the door.* TONY *comes in through the french window. They all watch* BEECHAM.)

LADY LISTER. Oh, Beecham.

BEECHAM. Yes, milady ?

LADY LISTER. Have you seen the newspapers this morning ?

BEECHAM. Not yet, milady, no.

TONY. You're billed to stand against me as a Tory in the by-election.

BEECHAM (*going out*). Very good, my lord.

TONY. Hey, Beecham.

(BEECHAM *stops.*)

(*Crossing upstage to* L.C.)   Just as well it's out.   It gives you time to knock this joker on the head and tell 'em you'll withdraw.

LADY LISTER.   You will withdraw, of course.   You couldn't want to stand.   And as it's clearly someone's joke, we'll say no more about it, will we, Joe ?

LORD LISTER.   No, rather not.   Except, of course, I hope you'll come and stay with us if you get in.

BEECHAM.   Most certainly.   I will accept with deepest gratitude, my lord.

LORD LISTER.   No, not a bit.   Be nice to have you—er—er— round the place.   (*He picks up* The Times.)

(BEECHAM *turns to go once more.*)

TONY.   Here, Beecham, show some sense.   You must withdraw.

BEECHAM.   My lord, my party comes before my personal preferments.   If I'm chosen by the people's representatives, I have no option but to hear their call.

JUNE.   Hear !   Hear !

BEECHAM.   Will that be all, milady ?

LADY LISTER.   I suppose so, yes.

TONY.   I hope you've got a thousand quid to chuck away.

BEECHAM.   Crusaders never want for cash, my lord.

(*He exchanges a look with* JUNE *and goes out.*)

TONY (*furiously, turning on* JUNE).   You're backing him.

JUNE.   So what ?   I don't see why the Labour boys should sit on all the money-bags.

TONY.   Why can't you go away ?

JUNE.   I guess I will, when Mr. Charles is IN.

LADY LISTER.   Oh, children, please !   Joe, really this is serious. We've only got one servant in the place——

LORD LISTER.   Good thing !   He won't be here to chuck the plates about.

LADY LISTER.   Oh, what a blessing Bessie's here.

TONY.   You won't have Bessie any more.   (*He sits on the* R. *arm of the sofa.*)

LADY LISTER   Why not ?   She hasn't given notice, has she ?

TONY.   No   I'll give it for her, Mother.   I've made up my mind.   I'm going to marry Bessie.

JUNE.   Tony !   You're NOT !

TONY.   I didn't think that it'd interest you.

JUNE.   You must be NUTS.

TONY.   O.K.   That's something you should understand.

(JUNE *snatches her engagement ring off, flings it at* TONY *and rushes from the room—down* L.—*in tears.   The ring falls in* LORD LISTER'S *sausages.*)

LORD LISTER (*picking it out*).   I say—the butcher forgot to take the ring out of this pig's nose !

LADY LISTER (*taking the ring from him*).   Oh, Tony dear, why must you talk like that ?   You've upset June.

TONY.   But, Mother dear, it's true.

LADY LISTER.   But, dear, we haven't got a servant in the place.

TONY.   I can't help that.

LADY LISTER.   Of course you can—you should have thought of that before you put the question, dear.   And Caroline and Lord Cleghorn are coming here the week-end after next.   Joe, Joe, DO SOMETHING, Joe !

LORD LISTER (*looking up from* The Times).   What is it, dear ?

LADY LISTER.   Tony says he wants to marry Bessie.

LORD LISTER.   Who's Bessie ?

TONY.   Bessie Sykes, Father.

LORD LISTER.   Ah, yes.   The girl who called that night about the Commonwealth.   Dashed pretty girl.   Does June agree ?

TONY.   I don't care what June thinks.

LADY LISTER.   But, Joe, Bessie's the maid.

LORD LISTER.   What maid ?

LADY LISTER.   Our maid.   She's BESSIE, dear.

LORD LISTER.   Well, that's all right, if Beecham doesn't mind.

LADY LISTER.   Oh, dear—you are so thoughtless, Tony.   You've got no idea how difficult they are to get.

LORD LISTER.   What ?   Maids or wives ?

LADY LISTER.   Now don't be silly, dear.   I'm really angry now. I'll have to ring the agency.

LORD LISTER.   Now stop it, Moll.   You married me.   Why shouldn't Bessie Sykes get married too ?   Where's June ?

TONY.   In hell, I hope.

LADY LISTER.   Tony, I will not have that talk.   You've upset June, you've upset me.   (*Rising.*)   I'll have to go and comfort her. You really are too thoughtless, dear.   (*Crossing* L.)   Why these things have to happen when my ducks want feeding, I don't know.

(*She exits down* L.)

TONY (*moving down* L.).   Well, I must go and get the car—I've got to hand my nomination in by ten.

LORD LISTER.   You taking Beecham with you ?

TONY.   Damn it, no.

LORD LISTER.   You must.   I'm dashed if I'll send two cars these days.   (*He rises, crosses* L. *and rings the bell above the fireplace.*) I'll have him ready on the mat.   It's only civil, after all.

(TONY *goes out.   There is a pause.   Then* BESSIE *comes in to clear the breakfast and answer the bell.*)

BESSIE.   Did you ring, my lord ?

LORD LISTER.   Er—yes.   Is Beecham there ?

BESSIE. He's changing. Says he's going with Lord Pym, my lord.

LORD LISTER. Ah—yes. Ah—good. (*He watches her nervously as she clears the table, then summons up courage and walks across to her.*) Er—are you Bessie—eh?

BESSIE. Yes, my lord.

LORD LISTER (*putting out his hand*). I'm Lister. How d'you do? I hope you'll come and stay with us as soon as you can get away——

BESSIE (*bewildered*). Thank you, my lord.

LORD LISTER. You give your fortnight's notice in to-day and come and stay the week-end of the poll.

BESSIE (*still more bewildered*). What, my lord?

LORD LISTER. Er—aren't you Bessie Sykes?

BESSIE. I am, my lord.

LORD LISTER. That's right—I thought you were. Well, you're engaged to Tony.

BESSIE. Me!

LORD LISTER. Yes—hasn't he told you yet?

BESSIE. He hasn't, no, my lord.

LORD LISTER. Oh, well, perhaps he forgot. My family's very absentminded. Still, you can take it from me you are engaged. Congratulations. We'll have a lot of fun. Well, I'm afraid I must go now. Er—yes. Excuse me. I've got to go and feed those blasted ducks.

(*He goes out down* L. BESSIE, *rather stunned, turns once more to the table. Then* BEECHAM *enters down* L., *wearing* LORD LISTER'S *very loud suit*—LORD LISTER'S *St. James's Street hat in hand.*)

BEECHAM. Now, lunch at one—if I'm not back—and keep your place—and say ' my lord '—and get the silver cleaned, you understand?

BESSIE. Yes, Mr. Beecham, very good.

BEECHAM. I'll trouble you to call me Mr. Charles.

BESSIE. Yes, Mr. Charles.

BEECHAM (*at the fireplace, taking a cigar out of his pocket and lighting it*). And don't let's have you breaking any plates. This place is not a music hall.

BESSIE (*turning on him*, L.C.). Don't talk to me like that! I'm going to marry Tony.

BEECHAM (*shaken out of himself*). You're what?

BESSIE. I'm going to marry Tony, so don't you talk to me like that—and learn to keep *your* place.

TONY (*off*). Beecham!

BEECHAM (*in a strangled voice which* TONY *does not hear*). Yes, my lord.

TONY (*shouting louder*). BEECHAM!

BEECHAM (*drawing himself up to his full height, hat on head, cigar in mouth, defiant*).   Comin', Pym.

(*Majestically and slowly he goes out, down* L).

CURTAIN

ACT III

SCENE 1

The day of the by-election count. Before lunch—a fortnight later,
BESSIE, *staying here now, is alone and bored. In her ' Sunday
best,' she is seated at* R. *end of the sofa, reading* The Tatler, *which
she has obviously read several times before. She throws it down
beside her, looks at the telephone, then at the clock and hurries to
turn on the news.*
The voice of the RADIO ANNOUNCER *comes through.*

RADIO ANNOUNCER. This was denied by the Ministry of Food
to-day.

(BESSIE *is about to switch off when she hears the following.*)

The result of the East Milton by-election has not yet been declared.
As listeners to our earlier bulletin were informed, there has already
been one re-count and another has been in progress all the morning.
There has also been a further examination of spoilt papers and the
result may be expected in the early afternoon.

(LORD LISTER *enters through the french window and stands listening.*)

Our correspondent understands that, while they are awaiting the
result, both candidates will be entertained to luncheon at Lister
Castle by the Earl of Lister who, as Lord Lieutenant, takes no part
in party politics. (*Pause.*) A second denial from the Ministry of
Food——

(BESSIE *switches off.*)

LORD LISTER. No news ?
BESSIE. He says ' expected in the early afternoon.' (*She moves
down and sits* R. *on the sofa again.*)
LORD LISTER. You seen my wife ?
BESSIE (*resuming* The Tatler). She's dishing up the luncheon, I
expect.
LORD LISTER. Does she know both of 'em are coming to lunch ?
BESSIE. Expect so. Everybody in the country seems to know.
LORD LISTER. Oh, yes, my dear. The B.B.C. knows everything.
They know it's going to rain before the weather knows itself. I
wish you'd run along and tell her what that fellow said—and help
her out a bit.
BESSIE. Oh, shucks. I helped her with the slops to-day.
LORD LISTER. Oh, really, did you ? I didn't know. That puts a
different light on it. All right, I'll go myself. (*He crosses down* L.
in front of the sofa.)

54

BESSIE.   You think I'm selfish, don't you ?

LORD LISTER.   What ? (*He stops.*) No, rather not. I see your point.   You mustn't overdo it on your first day as a guest.

BESSIE.   You think that's funny, don't you ?

LORD LISTER.   No, no.   Rather not.

BESSIE.   You do—you're laughing at me.   I can tell you it's—it's no fun staying here.

LORD LISTER.   By Jove, you've said a mouthful there.

BESSIE.   What ? You agree ?

LORD LISTER.   Of course I do.   I bet a galley-slave—if one came here to stay—would send himself a telegram.

BESSIE (*practically sobbing as the result of this unexpected sympathy*). And Tony wouldn't take me to the count.

LORD LISTER.   Oh, wouldn't he ? P'raps there wasn't room.

BESSIE.   There's room for June, so why not for me ?

LORD LISTER.   Ah, yes—why not ? I'd better slip along and——(*He starts for the door again.*)

BESSIE.   I'll tell you why he wouldn't take me.   He's ashamed of me, that's why. (*She starts sobbing.*) Oh dear, I wish I was a maid again.

LORD LISTER (*startled*).   My dear, you don't mean . . . ? Oh, yes, yes.   A maid.

BESSIE.   At least I got two pounds a week.   And had an overall to wear.   Now everybody wants me to keep on working—every minute—in my Sunday best, without a single penny for my pains. It isn't fair.

LORD LISTER.   Come, come, my dear.   We all get used to it in time. (*He moves to the sofa and sits* L. *of* BESSIE.)

BESSIE.   I won't.   I never won't.

LORD LISTER.   Oh, yes—you will.   The first initial shock—when one starts roughing it—is always worst.   I know it from experience. The army taught me that.   It doesn't last, my dear.   We human beings are adaptable, you know.   And Nature helps us to adjust ourselves to all the trials we have to face through life. (*He is getting a little involved, so he pats* BESSIE's *head*.) There, there, my dear. I wish that I were younger.   Fifty years ago I would have known the way to brush away those tears.   I've not forgotten yet, by Jove. (*He moves away from temptation, however, rises, goes to the radio table and picks up a book.*) Here, have a look at that.   It's interesting. It traces rabbits from the Ice Age down to 1939.

(*Nodding kindly to* BESSIE, *he goes out down* L.   BESSIE *flings the book away across the floor to* R.C. *The door-bell rings.   She rises and picks it up again.* LADY CAROLINE *and* LORD CLEGHORN *are heard off* L.)

LADY CAROLINE (*off*).   What an extraordinary thing.   There must be someone in.

LORD CLEGHORN (*off*).   Perhaps they've all gone off to hear the count.

LADY CAROLINE (*off*).   Whatever for ?

LORD CLEGHORN (*off*).   Morbidity.   To see the last Conservative brought low.

(LADY CAROLINE *enters down* L., *followed by* LORD CLEGHORN.)

LADY CAROLINE (*coming in*).   My dear Lord Cleghorn, you're counting chickens before they're hatched.   (*Crossing* R.C. *to* BESSIE.) Ah !   Here's Bessie, at any rate.   Lord Cleghorn—this is Bessie. I've heard all about you from dear Molly, and I've told Lord Cleghorn EVERYTHING.

BESSIE.   How do you do ?

LORD CLEGHORN (*not shaking hands*).   I think we met a few week-ends ago ?

BESSIE.   Yes.   I think we did.

LORD CLEGHORN.   I think Lady Caroline would like to see her room.

LADY CAROLINE (*just as* BESSIE *starts scowling*).   I know my room. I always have the Purple Room.   I've had it since I was a tiny girl. I wonder which is yours.

LORD CLEGHORN.   I'm sure Bessie will conduct me there.

BESSIE.   Here—don't you start on me as well.   (*Putting the book down on the desk.*)   I'm staying here, like you.

LORD CLEGHORN.   So I perceive.   But still, I thought you might be ready to assist a fellow guest to find his room.

(BESSIE *stamps her foot and goes out of the french window.*)

I call that most uncalled for.   What a very common, vulgar little girl.

LADY CAROLINE.   I think she's rather sweet.   She'll polish up quite wonderfully.   She's just uncut.   (*She sits in the armchair.*)

LORD CLEGHORN (*wincing*).   She doesn't know her place.   (*He sits* R. *on the sofa.*)

LADY CAROLINE.   Does anyone, these days ?

LORD CLEGHORN.   Yes, I do.   I'm plebeian—and I'm proud of it.

LADY CAROLINE.   What—proud of what you were ?   Or what you are to-day ?

LORD CLEGHORN.   Of what I was, of course.

LADY CAROLINE.   And not of what you are ?

LORD CLEGHORN.   I didn't say that.

LADY CAROLINE.   I think you're just proud.   And that's a failing you must try to cure.

LORD CLEGHORN.   I like that !   You're far the proudest person I have ever met.

LADY CAROLINE.   I'm getting less proud every day.   I'd like to be like Joe.   He's got no pride at all.   I sometimes think that that's the highest state we mortals can attain.   The greatest quality tradition has to offer to the world. One generation can't achieve it, though. It's handed down and—thank the Lord—it can't be taxed.

(LORD LISTER *comes in through the french window with a basket of potatoes.* LORD CLEGHORN *rises.*)

LORD LISTER (*coming down* C.). Hullo, Caroline. Hullo, Cleghorn. Sorry that I wasn't here to meet you. I've been getting some spuds. Been down to the Town Hall ?

LORD CLEGHORN. No—we came straight here from the station.

LORD LISTER. Ah, yes—yes, I see. A fellow told us—on the B.B.C.—that both of 'em are coming back to lunch. Dashed nice of him. Re-count, you know.

LORD CLEGHORN. Re-count ! I can't believe it !

LORD LISTER. Well, there it is. Dashed funny things, re-counts. You count the votes once, and you reach a certain total—if you follow me. Then, dashed if you don't count 'em again—and you're hundreds out. Uncanny. How do you explain it, Cleghorn, eh ?

LORD CLEGHORN. I can only hazard the suggestion that someone counts them wrong.

(BEECHAM *enters down* L., *wearing a blue rosette.*)

LORD LISTER. Ah, here you are. Er—Cleghorn, do you know—er—dash it, Beecham, what's your name to-day ?

BEECHAM. Benjamin Charles, my lord.

LORD CLEGHORN. How do you do ?

BEECHAM. Extremely well, my lord.

LORD CLEGHORN. Good weather for a by-election, eh ? (*He sits* R. *on the sofa again.*)

BEECHAM. A Tory sun is peeping fitfully through Labour clouds, my lord.

(BESSIE *comes in through the french window.* BEECHAM *regards her with distaste.*)

LORD LISTER (*to fill the breach*). We heard the news. There wasn't any.

BEECHAM. The agent will ring through, my lord, if the result comes through earlier than expected.

LORD LISTER. Is June back yet ?

BEECHAM. Miss Farrell is photographing Labour Party slogans chalked on the paintwork of the car, my lord.

LORD CLEGHORN. Good reading, I'll bet.

BEECHAM. I hardly think that statements like ' Old Beecham's heading for the House of Lords as well,' will earn immortal fame in English literature, my lord.

LORD CLEGHORN. How bigoted these people are. Provided that a man can get things done, I have no quarrel with the heights to which he may attain. They never seem to understand that leader-

ship's a quality that's only granted to the lucky few, and then it
rightly gains its own reward.

BEECHAM. Exactly so, my lord. (*To* LADY CAROLINE.) I'll
take your suitcase up, my lady.

LADY CAROLINE. Please don't bother—I can manage it.

(LADY LISTER *enters down* L., *wearing an apron.* LADY CAROLINE
and LORD CLEGHORN *rise.*)

LADY LISTER (*crossing to* C.). Dear Caroline—how well you look.
(*Turning to* LORD CLEGHORN.) How are you ? Sorry that I wasn't
here to meet you, but I couldn't leave the vegetables.

BEECHAM. What vegetables, my lady ?

LADY LISTER. Mostly Brussels sprouts, I think. (*She moves to
above the sofa.*)

BEECHAM. Here, Bessie—— (*there is a tense hush*) —you hop
along and watch the veg. Her ladyship has other things to do.

BESSIE. Pipe down. I'm staying here.

BEECHAM (*quietly*). You heard me, Bess. (*He opens the door
for her.*)

(BESSIE *crosses and exits down* L., *breaking into a run as she passes the
masterful* BEECHAM. LORDS LISTER *and* CLEGHORN *avoid each
other's eye.*)

Nicely done Brussels sprouts are one of the minor rewards of
leadership, my lord. Your lordship's room is next door to the
Purple Room.

LADY CAROLINE (*crossing* L.). Come along with me. I know
where it is. I'll show it to you, Jackie.

(*She goes out down* L.)

LORD LISTER. Who's Jackie ?

LORD CLEGHORN (*embarrassed*). My name is Jackie.

BEECHAM. I'll take your bags up, my lord.

LORD CLEGHORN. No, no, rather not. You stay here.

(*He goes out down* L.)

LORD LISTER. Well, dash it—I'd say that fellow was in love
with Caroline—if I didn't know she'd got a face like the back of a
bulldozer.

LADY LISTER. Joe—*pas devant* . . .

(BEECHAM *moves up* L.)

LORD LISTER. Eh, what—*pas* who ?

LADY LISTER. Oh, Joe, be quiet.

LORD LISTER. I won't be quiet. You started it by saying Pas
somebody. What the devil is it ?

LADY LISTER. Joe, I said BE QUIET.

(*She goes out in anger, down* L.)

LORD LISTER (*mystified*). Well, I'm dashed. She's like a scalded cat. Have I done something wrong ?

BEECHAM. Her ladyship was talking French, my lord.

LORD LISTER. She can't talk French.

BEECHAM. Her ladyship did not attempt the accent, I admit, my lord. She merely phrased the first two words of the French idiom (*with a beautiful accent*) *pas devant les domestiques.*

LORD LISTER. What the devil does it mean ?

BEECHAM. A hackneyed phrase, my lord—denoting that the subject mooted by some member of the company is scarcely fitted for the servants' ears.

LORD LISTER. Oh, that was it. Oh, thanks. What was the subject, eh ?

BEECHAM. Your lordship merely stated that your sister, Lady Caroline—in your opinion—lacked those qualities that might have launched a Trojan war, my lord.

LORD LISTER. Well, nothing wrong with that.

(*The telephone rings. BEECHAM crosses to it. JUNE passes the window up C. and enters.*)

JUNE. Say, is this IT ?

(*JUNE moves towards the telephone, but BEECHAM forestalls her.*)

BEECHAM (*in his butler's voice*). Hullo, sir ? . . . Yes, sir. Hold the line a moment, sir, and I will see if he's in.

LORD LISTER. Who is it—me ?

BEECHAM. No. It's the Press for me, my lord.

LORD LISTER. Well, get on with it, man.

(*He crosses and exits down L. with the potatoes.*)

BEECHAM (*at the telephone—the politician's voice*). Hullo, yes . . . I am Mr. Charles . . . An article ? Hold on. I'll put you through to my secretary. (*He calls near the mouthpiece.*) Miss Farrell.

JUNE (*near the telephone*). O.K., Mr. Charles. (*Into the telephone.*) Yeah—yeah . . . She's speaking . . . An article. O.K. What's its worth ? . . . What, fifty pounds ? What's that in dollars ? . . . Hell—that's chicken feed. Say, listen, do you know we've got a lot to do ? We can't waste time on parish magazines . . . I don't care what Lord Beaverbrook says. It's what I say that goes around these parts . . . A hundred. Yeah. O.K. Well, cheery-bye . . . So long, white slave. (*She rings off, sits at the desk and takes pencil and paper.*) O.K., Ben, let's do it now. Say, are you pro- or anti-war ?

(*BEECHAM looks bewildered.*)

BEECHAM. What is this about, then, miss ?

JUNE. Foreign policy. Sorry, I thought you knew.

(*BEECHAM goes to the table above the sofa.*)

BEECHAM. A glass of sherry, miss?

JUNE. No, thanks. Have one yourself. It might ease up the joints.

BEECHAM (*pouring one out*). Will you please take this down, miss.

(*He takes a sip of sherry.* TONY *comes in down* L. *and stands regarding* BEECHAM *with distaste.*)

I do not believe in wars . . .

JUNE. Say, let's have something definite. That's wind.

BEECHAM. All politicians tend to vaporize a little, miss. (*Continuing with a slightly diminished confidence.*) I do not believe in wars . . . (*Pause.*) I do not believe in wars . . .

TONY. You've said that just three times.

(BEECHAM *puts down his sherry and draws himself up.*)

BEECHAM. No doubt your lordship finds it hard to visualise a politician saying anything identical on three consecutive occasions.

TONY. Carry on.

BEECHAM. I believe—— (*To* JUNE.) If you'll excuse me, miss, I do not find the atmosphere conducive to developing my thesis for a working foreign policy. I think I'll go and find a less congested area in which to work. (*He crosses to the french window.*)

TONY. Yes, good idea.

BEECHAM (*stopping on his way out*). Would your lordship care to have a sporting wager on the outcome of the count? I'll lay you nine to four against yourself, my lord.

TONY. Dashed cocky, aren't you?

BEECHAM. Quietly confident, my lord. I'll give you three to one.

TONY. Shut up—you make me sick. (*He moves to the sofa and sits on the* L. *arm.*)

BEECHAM. I offer my apologies, my lord. I always understood finance was uppermost in every Labour politician's mind.

(*He stalks out through the french window.* JUNE *rises and moves* C.)

JUNE (*after a pause*). Tony.

TONY. Hullo—on speaking terms again?

JUNE. On any terms you like. Please don't be angry, Tony. I just did it 'cos I love tradition and—and all the things you really love and don't quite know you do.

TONY. Then you'd better get around to loving Bessie too.

JUNE (*attempting a light laugh*). Oh, Bessie. She's a silly thing. I don't mind that.

TONY. That's big of you.

JUNE. I know you only did it 'cos you lost your rag. I don't mind that. There's no harm done. It won't hurt you. It won't hurt her—because she's just a silly little flirt.

TONY (*losing his temper—rising*). She's not a flirt. She isn't silly. She's a damn sight more intelligent than you.

JUNE (*losing her temper as well*). Oh, yeah? She is? O.K. Well—marry her. Go on and marry her.

TONY. I'm going to. It'll be in the papers when this dashed result is out. Is that O.K. by you?

JUNE. O.K.—that's swell. (*She is hysterical now.*) You marry her—and have your sausages half done. Go on and marry her—and eat your lousy half-cooked sausages.

TONY (*shouting, as he crosses up* R.). Why don't you go back to the States and stop this bloody row?

(*He goes out through the french window.*)

JUNE (*shouting too*). O.K.—I will. (*She rushes to the telephone.*) Hullo! Hullo! I want the American Embassy, London . . . Yeah. I'll hold the line . . .

(BESSIE *enters down* L. *and moves up to above the sofa.*)

Yeah, yeah. United States Embassy, Grosvenor Square, London, England. Yeah.

BESSIE. I hope you're not sore about Tony. After all, a man's allowed to change his mind. (*She takes the election magazine from the table up* R.C.)

JUNE. I guess he is. Provided he's got a mind to hand in in exchange.

BESSIE. Here, give a girl a chance. You don't get much in life if you're a parlourmaid. It's " Yes, my lord," the whole damn beastly day.

JUNE. I guess you might try giving ' No, my lord ' a break. (*To telephone.*) Hullo, yeah—that the Embassy? . . . Oh, Mr. Rogers, please . . . Say, that you, Bolles? June Farrell here. Say, listen, Bolles. I want a passage to the States . . . Right now . . . Say, when's she sail? . . . To-morrow, that's O.K. You do your best and ring me back at once. Lister one—O-N-E . . . No, I can't hold on . . . (*Angrily.*) No, sir—I'm *not* a bride.

(LORD LISTER *enters down* L., *just as* JUNE *slams down the telephone.*)

LORD LISTER. Lunch is nearly ready. Where is everyone? (*To* BESSIE, *who is reading* BEECHAM'S *election address.*) Hullo—you going Tory, Bessie? Dashed good stuff. (*He crosses to the french window and calls through.*) Hey, Tony, lunch is nearly ready.

TONY (*off*). All right, Dad. I'm coming.

(LADY CAROLINE *and* LORD CLEGHORN *enter down* L.)

LORD LISTER (*crossing to the sofa table*). Now, Cleghorn, have a drink.

(JUNE *moves in to* R.C.   TONY *enters through the french window and comes down. The telephone rings.* TONY *picks up the receiver.*)

TONY. Pym speaking—are you the Town Hall ? . . . What ? . . . Who's still on the line ? . . . The American Embassy ? . . . What's that ? . . . The Washington ? . . . Southampton. Nine o'clock. To-morrow night . . . Yes. I'll tell her . . . Thanks. Good-bye. (*He hangs up and turns round to* JUNE.)

JUNE. O.K. I got the message, thanks. (*She crosses quickly* L.)

TONY. June——

(JUNE *exits down* L. *During the above,* LORD LISTER *has handed sherry to* LADY CAROLINE *and* LORD CLEGHORN, *who are by the fireplace. He is now determined to cheer things up.*)

LORD LISTER. Reading your election address in bed last night, Tony. All this talk about capitalism. Dashed rot. Every country's a capitalist country. Just depends whether it's state capitalism or private capitalism, that's all.

CLEGHORN. Exactly—that's our point.

LORD LISTER. But it isn't the point. The dashed point is— whether the private owner or the state are bigger crooks.

LADY CAROLINE. Joe, don't forget you take no part in party politics.

LORD LISTER. That isn't party politics. It's common sense.

(*The telephone rings.*)

That damn thing ought to be cut off. (*He gets there first.*) Hullo ? . . . Yes, Brown . . . You're speaking from the Town Hall ? . . . What ? . . . You've got the result and you want a pencil ? Surely to God you didn't ring me up for a pencil !

(JUNE *enters through the french window.*)

(*In response to various offers.*) No—no—he's got a pencil at the Town Hall. (*Into the telephone.*) Ye-es. I see. You know, of course, I take no part . . . You do ? But I'll gladly pass it on to 'em . . . Yes . . . Thanks. (*A thought strikes him.*) Oh, Brown— I'd like to see you sometime. Any time you're free. About these damn foxes—there are too many of them. I thought we might have a shoot. The Master's in the South of France—so now's the time . . .

(*Tension is almost at breaking point.*)

Yes, come and dine one night and we'll have a chat . . . Yes, yes— I'll tell 'em both. Good-bye. Damned good of you to ring up. (*He hangs up.*) Now, Tony, where were we ?

JUNE. Joe—did he say who won ?

LORD LISTER. Yes—rather—yes.

JUNE. Well—WHO ?

LORD LISTER. What ? Well, what did he say ? Er—dammit, you confuse me so. (*He goes and sits at* L. *end of the sofa.*)

(LORD CLEGHORN *crosses to the telephone and lifts the receiver.*)

LORD CLEGHORN. The Town Hall, please, at once . . .

LORD LISTER (*during the wait for the call*). I know he wants to tell somebody——

LORD CLEGHORN. Hullo . . . Lord Cleghorn—Lister Castle— here. Have you the result ? . . . I thank you . . . Many thanks. Good-bye. (*He hangs up.*) Your butler won by thirty votes.

BESSIE (*coming* C. *and breaking the hush*). Oh, goodie. And I voted for him, too.

TONY. You—WHAT ?

BESSIE. I voted for him 'cos Mum said you was a Bourgeois.

TONY. This is the end. I'd like to meet a consistent woman for a change.

LORD CLEGHORN (*chivalrously pointing to* JUNE). Well, this is one. (*Going to* JUNE.) Congratulations. You must be feeling very happy now.

JUNE (*looking up for the first time since the news came through*). Oh, God ! I wish we had lost !

(*She bursts into tears and goes and rests her head on* LORD LISTER'S *shoulder. He accepts the position with mingled pleasure and embarrassment.*

The door down L. *opens and* BEECHAM *enters. Momentarily dismayed by the scene before him, he forgets that he is a guest bearing a message to other guests and, despite his rosette, becomes the butler again.*)

BEECHAM. Luncheon is served.

LORD LISTER (*to* JUNE). Excuse me, please. (*He gets up and goes to* BEECHAM.) Ah, Beecham, just in time. Come in, come in, my dear fellow. (*He takes him by the arm.*) I want you all to meet our new M.P. My sister Caroline ; Lord Cleghorn ; your opponent you know ; Miss Sykes and Miss Farrell. May I congratulate you from us all ?

(*There is an unhappy lack of response to this gesture.*)

Now come along and meet my wife.

(*He urges him happily towards the door as
the* CURTAIN *falls.*)

ACT III

SCENE 2

Later the same night.

LORD LISTER *and* LORD CLEGHORN *are at the table* R.C., LORD LISTER *pouring out three glasses of port.* BEECHAM *is standing aloof up* L. *All are wearing the same clothes as in the previous scene. Cigars have been lighted.*

LORD LISTER. Dash it—I wish Molly wouldn't pull the table cloth away before I've had my port. I feel like a displaced person.

LORD CLEGHORN (*sitting in the armchair*). Still, you've got a lot to be thankful for. Your wife's a wonderful cook.

LORD LISTER. Think so ? I didn't think that bit of salmon was born yesterday. Here, have a glass of port. Who the devil are these glasses for ? I must be getting like those fellows at the count who couldn't count. I wonder why the devil I brought three.

(*In the background* BEECHAM *shifts awkwardly—unseen.* LORD LISTER *sits down on the chair* C., *dismissing the matter from his mind. He and* LORD CLEGHORN *each take a glass.*)

Talking about salmon, Cleghorn—their sex life, my dear fellow— quite astonishing. Do you know—the female spawns—and then the male comes along later—when she isn't there, mark you—never meet. Extraordinary ! Imagine, my dear fellow ! For the sake of argument, my sister Caroline—stayed at Claridge's one night— you know, passing through, shopping and so forth—and then you— or any dashed fellow for that matter, up for a board meeting—stayed there the next night. Well—see what I mean ? If you were a salmon—both of you, of course—dashed if the manager wouldn't find his dashed hotel half full of little silver smolts !

BEECHAM. I've always understood that some ninety per cent. of the male fish—after the—er—spawn is completed—fail to survive the long trip down river to the sea. (*He comes down* C.)

LORD LISTER. Very likely—overdo it, eh ? (*Suddenly realising that* BEECHAM *is present and has contributed the last remark.*) What the devil do you know about it, anyway ?

BEECHAM. The annual holiday, which you always assumed I spent at Blackpool with my bucket and spade, was, in reality, enjoyed on a Scottish river where I've leased a rod for more than thirteen years.

LORD LISTER. Well—I'll be—— Think you might have told me. Crazy about fishing, after all.

BEECHAM. Exactly, my lord, and it has always been my ambition to assimilate sufficient capital to lease another rod and to invite you as my guest.

LORD LISTER. That's very decent of you. Very decent. Let me see, they hope to raise the M.P.'s salaries this session, don't they, Cleghorn, eh ?

LORD CLEGHORN. I've heard the subject mentioned, certainly.

LORD LISTER. Oh, good. Here, Beech—er, Charles, do go and get yourself a glass of port. Expect you've got the cellar key.

(BEECHAM *makes towards the door down* L. *in embarrassment.*)

LORD CLEGHORN (*tactfully*). I think the port's already on the table, isn't it ?

LORD LISTER. Eh, what ? Yes—dash it—of course—that glass.

(*To* BEECHAM'S *retreating form.*) Beecham ! Here—come here. Sit down and have a glass of port.

BEECHAM (*coming to the table*). Thank you, my lord. (*He takes the third glass.*)

LORD CLEGHORN. Good health !

(*They all drink.* BEECHAM *takes his port to the sofa and sits. There is an awkward silence, broken by :—*)

LORD CLEGHORN. I can't help thinking of June Farrell, Lister.

LORD LISTER. Don't blame you. Dashed attractive, isn't she ?

LORD CLEGHORN. No, no, you get me wrong. I'm sorry that she's going. Though I disagree with her, of course—by gad, she's got some guts.

LORD LISTER. All of us have, my dear fellow. Do you know, if you tied one end of your gut—the greater gut, I think it's called—to, well we'll say, for the sake of argument, the middle stump at Lord's —you could walk down to the other end, shake hands with the bowler, and back—round the square-leg umpire—to the wicket ? No trouble at all, my dear fellow. Quite interminable. Hard to visualize. I mean to say—take Caroline—thin as a lead pencil— you'd never imagine . . .

LORD CLEGHORN. I can think of nothing Lady Caroline reminds me of less.

LORD LISTER (*interested*). Than what ?

LORD CLEGHORN. A pencil.

LORD LISTER (*mystified*). Who's talking about pencils ?

LORD CLEGHORN. I thought you were.

LORD LISTER. No, no. Caroline—you know, the one that's washing up.

LORD CLEGHORN. Yes, yes—I know.

LORD LISTER. Why are you looking at me like my bank manager ?

LORD CLEGHORN. I merely object to hearing a lady for whom I have the highest regard compared to a lead pencil.

LORD LISTER. Well—take my wife—no need to quarrel about her. Now, you'd never imagine to look at Molly that you could wind her round the Albert Hall, take her off to cocktails at the Ritz—without a break. (*He laughs.*)

(LADY CAROLINE *enters down* L., *taking off an apron. They all rise.*)

Hullo, Caroline. We've just been talking about you.

LADY CAROLINE. Oh, pulling me to pieces, I suppose. (*She moves up* L.) I've done the washing-up. Now June and Molly've started on the silver. And she wants you to do something to the boiler, Joe (*She puts the apron in the cupboard up* L.)

LORD LISTER. By Jove, yes. Needs a shot of coal. I don't know how to do it, though.

BEECHAM. Permit me to instruct you, then.

LORD LISTER (*as he passes* BEECHAM *on the way to the door*). No—not at all. You drink your port.

(*He goes out down* L. *with* LADY CAROLINE. LORD CLEGHORN *is left alone with Mr. Charles, M.P.*)

LORD CLEGHORN. Well, Beecham, how do you like being an M.P. ?

BEECHAM. I feel a little out of place, my lord.

LORD CLEGHORN. Oh, well, you've done a goodish job to-day— apart from all the repercussions in the house.

BEECHAM. You have no bitterness against me, then ?

LORD CLEGHORN (*going to him*). No—not a bit. Why should I have ? It's my profession—politics. You've done your job and done it well. But now it's done. (*He goes to the door.*)

BEECHAM. You say my job is done ?

LORD CLEGHORN (*turning*). Well, almost, yes. Not quite. (*He comes back to him.*) You'll never be a politician, Beecham. No professional at any job is any use in politics—Field Marshals, University Professors, Butlers—none of 'em are any good. You see, a politician does the odd-man's jobs. He lacks the concentration and integrity to specialize. So, Beecham, take my tip and don't degrade yourself. A man who has got a place in life should keep it.

BEECHAM. Then, what should I do ?

LORD CLEGHORN. Why don't you do what Lloyd George and Ramsay Mac—all their jobs completed—should have done ?

BEECHAM. What's that ?

LORD CLEGHORN. Resign. Goodnight.

(LORD CLEGHORN *goes out down* L.)

BEECHAM (*wistfully*). Resign !

(*He is left bewildered. Then* BESSIE *comes in through the french window.*)

And where have you been ?

BESSIE. Walking in the woods. (*She moves down and sits in the armchair.*)

BEECHAM. Alone ?

BESSIE. Of course I was alone. I've had this life. I'm through. Society makes me sick. God—it gets me down. Cold bath-water and moth-balls. I hope you done the washing-up to-night.

BEECHAM. It isn't proper for a man to do them dirty jobs.

BESSIE. My man'd have to do it.

BEECHAM. That's neither here nor there. Are you in love with Pym ? (*He goes to the table above the sofa and puts out his cigar.*)

BESSIE. Oh, I don't know.

BEECHAM. Don't you like me a little bit, Bess ?

BESSIE. I think you're very strong.

BEECHAM. Well then, don't strong men make fine handsome husbands for nice buxom country girls ?

BESSIE (*sitting up*). You asking me to marry you ?

BEECHAM. Strong men don't fall in love with butterflies. They kiss them sometimes, though. You hear me, Bess ? I said, " they kiss them sometimes, though."

BESSIE (*very quiet*). I heard you, Mr. Charles.

(*She turns her face round to him and he moves towards her. She then rises and breaks away in front of him to down* L.C.)

Don't, Mr. Charles. I couldn't never be a politician's wife. They gets above themselves.

BEECHAM (*following her down*). Who says I want to wed you ?

BESSIE. Who says you don't ? (*She kisses him all she knows.*) But you'll have to give up being an M.P. and learn to keep your place—that's straight.

(*She kisses him again.* LORD LISTER *comes in through the french window and coughs tactfully.* BESSIE *flies from the room, down* L.)

BEECHAM. Will you permit me to apologize ?

LORD LISTER (*moving down*). No, not at all. Still, Bessie seems to get around a bit. Correct me if I'm wrong, but she's engaged to Tony, isn't she ?

BEECHAM. The situation is a trifle fluid there. It could be solved by statesmanship.

LORD LISTER. Well, why not go ahead ?

BEECHAM. It needs self-sacrifice as well.

LORD LISTER. What rot ! (*He digs him in the ribs.*) If I was your age I'd know what to do. Go on, man—go on . . .

BEECHAM (*irresolute—suddenly decides*). Thank you, my lord.

(*He exits down* L. LORD LISTER *picks up his gun by the window and is going out as* TONY *comes listlessly in by the door down* L.)

TONY. Dad——

LORD LISTER (*off*). I've gone out.

(TONY *sits down on the sofa as* JUNE, *in her dressing-gown, peeps round the door to see if he is there—and, seeing him, comes in.*)

JUNE (*crossing to the sofa*). I'm going in the morning.

(*He doesn't answer.*)

Write to me, Tony. We've been good pals. You used to like me, Tony. I'm going to kiss you just once more for memory. (*She does—not very successfully.*) I'm sorry, Tony dear, you are Conservative. It's in your blood. It's in your family. It's in your heritage. I know I've lost you, Tony. I was silly. You were stronger-minded than I thought . . . You need your hair cut, Tony dear. (*Emotion overcomes her.*) Say something, please. (*Des-*

pairingly, crossing up to the window.)   I can't live without you, Tony.
I'm not going to live without you, do you hear ?   I'm going to die.
(*She rushes to where* LORD LISTER *keeps his rifle.*)   I'm going to shoot
myself.   Oh, Tony, don't you want to say good-bye ?

TONY.   No.   See you at the funeral.

(JUNE *reaches behind the curtain for the rifle.   A shot rings out.   She
screams.* TONY *rushes to her.*)

Oh, June.   My darling June.   You aren't hurt, are you ?

JUNE.   No.   That was Joe, I guess.

TONY.   June, my darling, will you marry me ?

JUNE.   Yes, but you'll have to get that job.

TONY.   But, darling—I've been thinking, landowning's a full-
time job.   When Father's agent dies, I'll take his job and run the
good old place.   What say you, eh ?

JUNE.   That sounds all right.   How old's your father's agent ?

TONY.   Twenty-eight.   But he gets frightful colds.

JUNE.   Oh, Tony darling, you're hopeless.   P'raps that's why I
love you, though.

TONY.   Of course it is—and till then there's always politics.

JUNE.   You've had it as a politician, kid.

TONY.   Don't you believe it.   We Listers always come up more
than twice.

JUNE.   But where ?

TONY.   Don't be so practical.

(*They fall into each other's arms.* LORD LISTER, *with his rifle, enters
in high excitement through the french window.*)

LORD LISTER.   Tony, I've got it at last !   Saw it in the moonlight, by the cypress tree.   Dashed brute—it had a duck right in
its jaw.

(*He leaves his rifle by the window, crosses and rings the bell, then notices*
JUNE *and* TONY *still locked in each other's arms.*)

Every time I come in the room this sort of thing's going on.   Where's
Beecham ?   I wish he'd hurry up.

(TONY *and* JUNE *break up.* LORD LISTER *rings again.*)

I wish he'd come—the beast may not be dead.

JUNE (*moving to the desk*).   It's no use ringing, Joe.

LORD LISTER.   Why not ?

JUNE.   You know, Joe.   Beecham's our M.P.

(BEECHAM *enters down* L., *dressed as a butler.   There is an electric
silence.*)

BEECHAM.   You rang, my lord ?

LORD LISTER (*alone unmoved by* BEECHAM'S *change of costume*).
There's a fox and a duck under the cypress tree.   (*He moves in to
above the sofa.*)

BEECHAM.   Alive or dead, my lord ?

LORD LISTER.   Dead, damn it—fetch 'em quick—before they disappear.

BEECHAM.   Yes—very good, my lord.

(He goes out through the french window at the double.)

JUNE.   Joe ! Tony ! Why is Beecham dressed like that.?

LORD LISTER.   Like what ?

JUNE.   In tails.

LORD LISTER.   Well, p'raps he likes 'em. P'raps they keep him warm.

JUNE.   But, Joe, get hold of something, can't you ? Beecham's our M.P.

LORD LISTER.   What ? Dash it—so he is. See what you mean, —no top hat.

(BEECHAM *enters carrying the corpses.* LORD LISTER *hurries to examine them.*)

BEECHAM.   Here we are, my lord.

LORD LISTER.   An old vixen, by jove—that'll save a century of ducks.

BEECHAM.   The duck was in the snare, my lord.

LORD LISTER.   What ? Dammit—then you set the thing too high.

BEECHAM.   Unless the bird was moving *ventre-à-terre*, my lord.

JUNE (*butting in*).   Say, Benjy, why the uniform ?

BEECHAM.   My name is Beecham, miss. (*To* LORD LISTER.)   I wonder—might I have your lordship's leave to use the telephone ?

LORD LISTER.   Yes, rather—ringing up the ' Field ' or something, eh ? (*Fingering the fox.*)   Dashed lovely coat.

(BEECHAM *places the duck on the table* R.C., *then goes to the telephone and lifts the receiver.* JUNE *comes to above the armchair.* TONY *is above the sofa,* LORD LISTER *up* C. *with the fox.*)

BEECHAM.   Lister eight-nine, please, miss.

LORD LISTER.   If I had that cured, I doubt if Molly'd ever know it wasn't some dashed vermin from a Bond Street store.

(He goes out through the french window with the fox.)

BEECHAM (*at the telephone*).   Hullo ? . . . Is that the *Advertiser* ? . . . Take a story, please . . . ' Mr. Benjamin Charles, M.P., the newly-elected member for Milton East, has decided to abandon the uncertainty of public life in favour of the constancy and unrivalled glory of domestic bliss ' . . . Yes, this is Mr. Charles himself . . . No—I am not. I had a single port at ten o'clock. Hullo ? . . . Quote continues—' I understand that Viscount Pym will contest the ensuing by-election in the interests of the . . .' Hullo ? Hullo ? I've been cut off. (*He hangs up.*)

TONY (*moving* C.).   Dashed good of you to give it up.

BEECHAM.   No—not at all, my lord.   I feel that you will make an excellent M.P.   The lessons you have learnt will strengthen you on future platforms.

JUNE.   Tory platforms, eh ?

BEECHAM.   Not necessarily—no.   I have lately come to the conclusion that provided one's personality is proved, the party one belongs to is quite immaterial, my lord.

JUNE.   Oh, Tony—now you've got a job, I will marry you.   (*She goes to him* C.)

TONY (*still worried*).   I've got to put things right with Bessie first.

BEECHAM.   You need anticipate no trouble on that score, my lord. She has found no difficulty in wiping the whole incident from her mind.

TONY (*stung*).   Oh !   Still—I'd better see her.

JUNE.   I think I'll come and hold your hand.

(*They go out down* L.   LORD LISTER *comes running in through the french window.*)

LORD LISTER.   Beecham, what about this second rod ?

BEECHAM.   The money paid by avid newspapers will cover that, my lord.

LORD LISTER.   It will, by Jove ?

(BESSIE *has entered, dressed once more as a maid.*)

BEECHAM.   I trust your lordship and her ladyship will come to Scotland as (*he includes* BESSIE) OUR guests.

LORD LISTER.   By gad, yes.   When ?

BEECHAM.   Next month, my lord, if we may take our honeymoon and holiday combined.   (*He has again included* BESSIE *in a sweeping and possessive gesture.*)

LORD LISTER.   Of course you can.   Dashed decent of you. Thanks.

BEECHAM.   The pleasure will be ours, my lord.

LORD LISTER.   Er—Beecham, er—does Bessie fish ?

BEECHAM.   Not with rod and line, my lord.

LORD LISTER.   Ah—dashed good girl.   (*He catches sight of the duck, turns it to examine the profile and recognizes it with horror.*) My God—it's Clara !   (*Running across in front of* BESSIE *to the door down* L.)   Molly !   Molly !

(*He runs from the room to own up to his wife.*)

BEECHAM (*moving* C. *and opening his arms to* BESSIE).   I've come to the conclusion that an odd-man's job is far beneath my dignity.   An odd-man is an odd-man, whether he is a politician or he merely carries up the coals.   I have resigned my Seat.

BESSIE (*leaping into his arms*).   My darling Ben !

(BEECHAM *swings her off the ground and kisses her.   The telephone rings.   He puts her down and indicates the duck.*)

BEECHAM.   Will you take that luckless creature to the larder, love ?   (*He goes to answer the telephone.*)

(BESSIE *picks up the duck and starts to go, but half-way to the door stops to listen.*)

(*At the telephone.*)   Hullo ? . . . What ? . . . Yes ?   The *Advertiser* ? . . . Yes, I know—we were cut off . . . I am applying for the Chiltern Hundreds . . .   My dear young man, where is your education ? To apply for the Chiltern Hundreds is the only means whereby a sitting Member may resign his Seat—a Parliamentary privilege of which, in my opinion, far too few M.P.s avail themselves.   I shall apply to-morrow morning after I have done the washing-up.   (*He bows towards* BESSIE.)

(BESSIE, *hearing this surrender over the washing-up, flits away triumphant, down* L.)

My resignation is a purely personal affair.   The policy has triumphed —and that is the point . . . What is that ? . . . What is my policy ? (*Indignantly he draws himself to his full height.*)   My policy is this. It is embodied, always and forever, in the phrase—" They also serve who only stand and wait."   Goodnight.

(*He hangs up the telephone, and moves with dignity towards his Destiny*—L.)

CURTAIN

FURNITURE AND PROPERTY PLOT.

ACT I

SCENE 1

Windows shut.
Curtains open.
Electric fittings OFF.

Door down L.
Fireplace L. :—*Accessories.*
Oil painting above fireplace.
Built-in cupboard up L. :—*Dustpan and brush ; duster.*
Lacquered bureau up L.C. (optional).
Large built-in bookcase C.
Table against bookcase :—*Tea chest (optional) ; radio ;* Radio Times *;
  magazines.*
Small table up R.C. :—Advertiser, *with quotation.*
Desk R. :—*Ornaments ; table lamp ; telephone ; ashtray ; blotter ; inkstand ;
  tray with pen and pencils ; notepaper : two letters to* CLEGHORN *; two
  envelopes to* CLEGHORN.
Portrait over desk.
Waste-paper basket above desk.
Sofa L.C. :—*Cushions.*
Table above sofa :—*Flowers in vase ; small lamp ; cigarette-box with
  cigarettes ; matches ; ashtray ; silver salver.*
Armchair R.C. :—*Rifle against* L. *arm ; cushion.*
Tobacco and match on floor by armchair.
Small table L. of armchair :—*Tobacco-jar with tobacco ; ashtray ; rabbit
  book.*
Three small chairs :—At desk, up R., and L. of window.

OFF L.

Tray for BEECHAM :—*Sherry ; four glasses.*

OFF R.

Rabbit for BEECHAM.

PERSONAL.

Pipe and matches for LORD LISTER
Spectacles for LADY LISTER (optional).
Blank cartridges for LORD LISTER.
Blue rosette for TONY.

SCENE 2

Windows open.
Curtains open.
Electric fittings OFF.

STRIKE.

Sofa table.
Duster from desk.
Rabbit book, tobacco-jar and ashtray from table R.C.

SET.

Sofa to new position up L.
Armchair to new position up R.C.
Small table R.C. to behind sofa.

Cigarette-box, ashtray and matches from sofa table to small table.
Lamp from sofa table to small table.
Flowers from sofa table to radio table.
Round breakfast table slightly R. of C.

> *Three places laid, each with:—napkin; two knives; fork; sideplate; cup,*
> *saucer and spoon.*
> *One place (LADY LISTER) laid with:—napkin; knife; dessert spoon; side-*
> *plate; plate of cereal; cup, saucer and spoon.*
> *Bread on platter and breadknife; toast in toast-rack; marmalade and spoon;*
> *butter and butter-knife; sugar and spoon; condiment set; three letters for*
> LADY LISTER; *silver basket.*

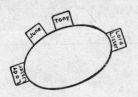

Three small chairs and one from offstage to breakfast table :—One L. for
LORD LISTER ; one R. for LADY LISTER ; two above table for JUNE and
TONY. N.B.—JUNE sits next to LADY LISTER, TONY between JUNE and
LORD LISTER. There is a larger gap between TONY and LORD LISTER
in order to make room for the coffee.
Trolley L.C., end up- and down-stage.

> *Hot plate, silver dish with three eggs on toast ; tray, three plates, serving*
> *spoon and fork ;* Daily Mail, Daily Express *and* The Times *on middle*
> *shelf.*

OFF L.

Coffee-pot with coffee, and milk jug with milk, for BEECHAM.
Plate of duck food for LORD LISTER.
Flashy novel for LORD LISTER.

OFF R.

Rabbit snare for LORD LISTER.

PERSONAL.

Cigarette-case with cigarettes, lighter, for TONY.

ACT II

SCENE 1

Windows open.
Curtains open.
Electric fittings ON.

SET.

Furniture as in Act I, Scene 1—EXCEPT :—
Armchair slightly towards C.
Small table R.C. to behind and R. of armchair :—*Lamp from sofa table ;*
one coffee-cup ; ashtray.
Chair from up R. to R. of small table.
One coffee-cup on floor by desk.

On desk :—*Flowers—changed since last Scene ; pile of opened letters ; one coffee-cup.*
On sofa table :—*Coffee-tray with pot, milk jug and two coffee-cups ; tray with whisky decanter, syphon of soda and seven glasses ; patience cards.*
On sofa :—*Work basket and mending.*
Check rifle in window.

OFF L.

Glass of water on salver for BEECHAM.

OFF R.

Crumpled *Advertiser* for BEECHAM.

PERSONAL.

Cigar and matches for CLEGHORN.
Cigarette-case with cigarettes for TONY.

SCENE 2

Windows open.
Curtains open.
Electric fittings OFF.

STRIKE.

Letters from desk.
Advertiser from table up R.C.

SET.

Furniture as in Act I, Scene 2.
Change flowers on desk.
Dish of undercooked sausages on trolley—NOT eggs on toast.
Duplicate engagement-ring on breakfast table, hidden by LORD LISTER'S sideplate.
Washer for JUNE to throw, hidden by JUNE'S sideplate.

OFF L.

Coffee-pot with coffee, and milk jug with milk, for BEECHAM.
Daily Mail, Daily Express and *The Times*, for BEECHAM.
Dish of well-cooked sausages for BEECHAM.

PERSONAL.

Cigar and matches for BEECHAM.

ACT III

SCENE 1

Windows open.
Curtains open.
Electric fittings OFF.

SET.

Furniture as in Act I, Scene 1.
Tray with sherry and four glasses on sofa table.
Rabbit book on radio table.
Tatler on sofa.
Vase of fresh flowers on radio table.
Election magazine on table up R.C.

OFF R.

Basket of potatoes for LORD LISTER.

PERSONAL.

Blue rosette for BEECHAM.
Red rosette for TONY.

SCENE 2

Windows open.
Curtains closed.
Electric fittings ON.

STRIKE.

Rabbit book from desk.
Tatler from sofa.
Sherry from sofa table, and glasses.

SET.

Furniture as in Act III, Scene 1—EXCEPT :—
Armchair and small table moved slightly to R.
Small chair from up.C. to L. of small table.
Desk chair pushed in.
Port bottle and three glasses on small table.
Rifle in window.

OFF R.

Fox and duck for BEECHAM.

PERSONAL.

Cigars each for CLEGHORN, LORD LISTER and BEECHAM.

EFFECTS

OFF L.

Motor horn and car.
Door bell.
Door slam.

OFF R.

Telephone bell.
Gun shot.

Any character costumes or wigs needed in the performance of this play can be hired from Charles H Fox Ltd, 25 Shelton Street, London WC2H 9HX.

MADE AND PRINTED IN GREAT BRITAIN BY
LATIMER TREND & COMPANY LTD PLYMOUTH